STAIRS OF LIFE

STAIRS OF LIFE

Neelam Singh

@Magicofbrands

Bigfoot Publications
Because, there's a writer in everyone.

Stairs of Life
Author : Neelam Singh

First Published by
Bigfoot06 Publications (OPC) Pvt. Ltd.
1st floor, BSR Building near Vishal Mega Mart,
Daultabad Flyover, Laxman Vihar Phase 3,
Gurugram, Haryana (122001)
Website: www.bigfootpublications.in
Email: info@bigfootpublications.in

First Edition : October, 2023

To contact with Neelam Singh for Motivational speaking arrangements, email : connect@neelamsingh.in

ISBN Print Book - **978-81-19512-63-8**

Printed in India

DEDICATIONS & ACKNOWLEDGEMENT

I am profoundly grateful to many individuals and organizations whose support, trust, and contributions made this book possible. Writing it has been an exciting journey and a learning experience filled with challenges and bliss.

My deep gratitude goes out to GOD, The Universe, Shrimad Bhagwat Geeta, My Parents, Sunny Nain (my better half), and Himani Sharma, my dear friend. Without them, I would not be able to do any of this. Thank you for believing in me and always being there for me.

I also extend my heartfelt thanks to my family and relatives, mentors, advisors, and friends for their love and support. I want to express my gratitude to my editors, research collaborators, my publisher, and all the professionals who helped shape this book.

And finally, I want to thank EVERYONE who came into my life and gave me all the life lessons, supported me, encouraged me, and all the critics who taught me about life.

To all my readers and supporters, I must say that I appreciate your enthusiasm and engagement. Your feedback and encouragement will always motivate me to strive for excellence.

Neelam Singh

PREFACE

Roy T. Bennett, in 'The Light in the Heart,' said, "Attitude is a choice. Happiness is a choice. Optimism is a choice. Kindness is a choice. Giving is a choice. Respect is a choice. Whatever choice you make makes you. Choose wisely."

So today, I make the choice to write this book, which I want to dedicate to the readers. I choose to motivate the people who are reading this and who have chosen to read the words that I will be writing inside. But before I start sharing some of my knowledge and experiences with you, let me tell you why I chose to write a book about it.

Writing a book is never as easy as it sounds in one's head. It took me two years to pick up my laptop and start typing my thoughts, and it took a lot of hard work to bring sense to those words. But more than that, this book was only possible because of all the years I have lived and the challenges I have faced in my life. I had to confront my share of the good and the bad, the happy and the unhappy, the stressful and the cheerful, and all the pleasant and unpleasant moments that life threw my way. Collecting all those experiences and the courage I gained from them, I write this book for you.

Before I share my story of reaching this stage in life, where I now run three startups and plan to expand further in the field of entrepreneurship, I want to share this saying by Confucius with you, my dear reader, '*The man who moves a mountain begins by carrying away small stones.*' And that's how I reached the mountain of my life.

It was never easy. I grew up in a village named Kaurali in Haryana and experienced city life only after completing my intermediate. I was an average student in my studies. After completing my 10th grade at ASN Senior Secondary School, I opted for Commerce in the 12th grade at Aggarwal Public School and pursued my graduation at D.A.V College. My family always dreamt of seeing me become a Chartered Accountant, so I took the path that could fulfill my family's dream. After completing my CA Articleship training with CA Harish Mangla & Associates, I shifted to Delhi for my CA final coaching, entering the bustling city life of Delhi, and the race to crack those exams began. I found myself surrounded by friends who were running the same race.

Like most students in Delhi preparing for CA and spending their crucial years living in the cramped areas of East Delhi, I too was stuck at the final stage of the exam. This led to frustration and sometimes motivation, but to be honest, getting stuck in life is disheartening.

The year 2020 brought horrific memories for people worldwide with the pandemic. I had to shift from Delhi back to my hometown, Faridabad, in Haryana. Prior to that, there had already been a drastic change in my mindset, and the best part was that I had already started working on my dream of becoming an entrepreneur.

In that phase, i was attended a business seminar of Mr. Ameet parekh . In that seminar one line hit me hard as they said to everyone, "If you want to start working on your dreams after 5 years, why don't you start it from today itself. Start now if possible because after 5 years you'll be 5 years ahead in respective profile from them who'll start after 5 years."

And here I started my first venture i.e ceNdor industry .

No one in the family knew about it except my mother. For them, I was still preparing for my CA exams. But once I took my business online and started to succeed, I had to finally tell my family that I no longer wanted to pursue a CA career. Hearts were broken, and hopes were shattered. However, they were still my family, and I am blessed to have them in my life. Their support and understanding gave me the strength to move forward and build a journey of my own. One thing my parents always said kept running through my mind: 'Don't worry. It's just an exam.' These words helped me break free from the cycle of exams and prevented me from falling into the abyss of depression.

And later I got selected from IIM Bangalore for entrepreneurship degree and got Goldman Sachs Entrepreneurship degree from IIM Bangalore .

One line that always keeps me positive in my life is that my father always tells me that "life is a game, just play well". Consider every phase of life as just A phase of life, do not consider that as the whole life.

So, in this book, I am going to share all that I have learned, from my teenage experiences of identity crisis and self-love to my startup days, where I got to work with the real world outside. Are you ready to discuss some of the common problems that you and I share? Let's find motivation through solutions to these everyday conundrums we all face in this book.

Table of Content

"7 Bridges of Success"

GRATITUDE

Someone very wise once said, "Gratitude turns what we have into enough".

With gratitude in life, you can count all those people and all those moments that matter the most. The people that provide value to your life and help you grow as an individual. Gratitude will help you recognize the VIPs (very important people) of your life who are there for you without being judgmental.

When you express gratitude towards what you have, you will always feel blessed. Feeling of gratitude will bring you closer to peace and your mind, body and soul can be put into things that are valuable to you and not the things that do not give you anything in return except unhappiness.

For instance, if you keep on complaining about what you do not have in life, will that bring those things and success in your life? Never. Instead, if you put your energy into being thankful for what you have will bring you closer to the things you truly deserve. Many people struggle to have a life like yours. Many people will struggle to have the peace that you can have with gratitude.

Some people assume that bringing gratitude into their life's means being closer to God. What if they do not believe in God? Gratitude has nothing to do with your faith or belief. You can even be grateful for your parents, or your friends who have been there for your support in your hard times. You can be grateful for those moments in your life, that gave you the best life lessons and evolved you from a naïve to a wiser person.

I discovered that gratitude works as magic in your life while I was reading the book 'The Magic'. I started giving myself 5 minutes daily and wrote down at the end of the day while going to sleep. I used to write these two questions and answered them daily. "What I was grateful for today?" and "What I could improve and do better tomorrow?". This worked as a best self-analysis, and I was able to bring the changes in my life that I always dreamt of but never got the push to work for them.

This analysis at the end of the day is my motivation to live my day and count all the good things that happen to me instead of wasting my time thinking about what wrong had happened to me.

If you can bring gratitude into your life, you can bring success too because you will be the person who focuses on the good and attracts only the best.

FORGET THE PAST

Steve Maraboli said these hard-hitting words, "Cry. Forgive. Learn. Move on. Let your tears water the seeds of your future happiness."

One thing I always tell people who regret their past is that they are wasting their time. Yes, you heard me right. Your past was a part of your life, and it was beautiful while you were living it. You can no longer relive those moments, but you can learn and move on to create more of them. The butterfly counts not months but moments and has time enough. Do not dwell in your past and waste the time you have in your present. Accept the fact that your PAST IS OVER. Some things can never be in our control, and then we regret thinking about them and not achieving anything from them in the end. Our past is one of those things, but our future is still in our hands if we focus only on the present. Work in your present and make the future beautiful again. Never predict your future based on your past experiences and stop living in the moment.

I know it is easy to say, 'live in the moment' because of YOLO. And I know you have one question right now: 'How to forget the past?' Meditate. Yes, meditate on it and forgive yourself for everything you think went wrong. Just forgive everyone and consider whatever happened as a lesson for life. Write it down somewhere—in your diary, or just send an email to yourself, penning down every emotion and very thought you have about your past and moving on from it.

Somewhere deep down, you know it wasn't right for you. Somewhere in your heart, you always had doubts, and that's why it is your past and not your present. The day you accept that and move on, you liberate yourself and choose to build a future that you deserve.

It is hard to forget, but forgiving will give you freedom. I know change is painful, and I too have gone through some pains of change, but life taught me that only change is growth. And if you no longer have those people you had in the past, or you no longer live the way you lived in the past, you have chosen to change and grow.

And as Eckhart Tolle said in 'The Power of Now,' "Time isn't precious at all, because it is an illusion. What you perceive as precious is not time but the one point that is out of time: the Now. That is precious indeed. The more you are focused on time—past and future—the more you miss the Now, the most precious thing there is."

MINDSET

When an elephant is small, the keeper puts a chain around his foot, and the baby elephant is not able to move out of it. But once the elephant grows old, the keeper still uses the chain to keep the elephant in place, even though it can easily break the chain and run away. The elephant does not do that. Do you know why? Because its mind has been conditioned from the time when the elephant was a baby that it cannot break those chains. The human mind works similarly.

You become what you feed your mind. And the best part about mindset is that you can change it anytime, at any stage of life. Mindset is all about what thoughts you keep in your head, and they will decide what you will attract the most in life. If you really want to change your life, relationship, or financial situation but do not want to change the way you think about it, nothing will ever change.

If you don't improve the way you think, you cannot improve the way your life works. There is a very famous line by

Paulo Coelho which goes like this, 'And when you want something, all the universe conspires in helping you to achieve it.' Think about what you want in life with a positive mindset.

If you think it's hard to change all at once, then take it slow, step by step. I never thought I would be able to write this book. I always had this dream of writing a book one day, but how? was the biggest question. I was never a daily reader until 2019 when my roommate, Himani, suggested I read daily even if I read a little. And once I got into the habit of reading, I have read more than 222 books so far. This brought me closer to my dream of writing a book one day. I now knew what it takes to write one and what the reader looks for in a book. This brought a change in my mindset, and here I am with a published book today.

All you have to do is apply the Next Mile concept from the book 'The Magic of Thinking.' I apply it to all my business projects and foundation (NGO) work. Set milestones for yourself and do it one by one. All you have to do is keep your thoughts about it positive, and you will see positive things coming around you. You will draw every resource you need to achieve your goals from around the universe.

Think what you want and change your mind about it, and the universe will make sure you get it. So always remember that the universe is listening. Think in the right way about yourself and your dreams because you will get what you think and not what you wish.

BELIEVE IN YOURSELF

"Be who you are and say what you feel, because those who mind, don't matter and those who matter, don't mind."

– Bernard M. Baruch

There was a point in my life where I had self-doubts about writing a book. In fact, there was a time when I had not even read a single book and never thought I would read so many. These doubts always stopped me from taking that first step toward writing. More and more doubts wanted to stop me from continuing to write.

But what I always told myself was if others can do it, so can I. That was my confidence, and if you are not thinking the same way, then maybe you need to rewire your brain to think positively about your capabilities because If I can, so can you.

You know there was a time when no one believed that Mount Everest could be climbed, but Bachendri Pal did and proved that her belief was stronger than all the negative ones. This proves that your belief in yourself is stronger than all the non-believers in you.

We all know that the lion is the king of the jungle because it believes so; otherwise, an elephant is bigger in size and strength. Your belief is what makes you a success or a failure. And no one wants to be the latter.

I benefited from many books like 'Believe in Yourself' and 'Awaken the Giant Within,' but the book I admired the most was 'Power of Subconscious Mind,' and I suggest you read it once in your life. It says that there is nothing like impossible in this world.

It's all in your head. I was preparing for my CA, and the future seemed bleak. My relatives had already started nagging my parents for marriage, but it was clear in my mind that I wouldn't marry until I did something for myself. I knew I would surely do it one day; that belief kept me going, and it was this same belief that has brought me to the ladder of success.

Similarly, you need to make up your mind and recognize your strength and USP (unique selling proposition). I would suggest that you read 'You're a Badass' if you carry a lot of doubts about yourself. In short, it tells about how your comfort zone creates fear in your mind, and ultimately self-doubt arises, which stops you from taking 100 percent action in your life.

I met a businessman, Sunny Nain, and while we were talking, he told me how he started his journey when he was in 11th standard in very adverse conditions, which are an excuse for some people. But at that age, he had the confidence and belief in himself to build an empire for himself that is a leading brand in Kitchen and home appliances, known as Superlex Appliances today. It is all about how you think about yourself in your head.

Stop saying negative things about yourself because the universe is listening, and it wants to prove everything you say is correct. So, say only good things so good things happen, and the universe conspires, as they say.

Whenever I faced confidence issues in my life, I always started by setting small targets that I could complete easily, so I could train my subconscious mind that things were happening, and I could do it. Start applying this in your life too, and you will find that your mind will itself start working to complete those targets.

For example: You set an alarm in the morning, and when it rings, you snooze it or turn off the alarm and go back to sleep. But when you wake up, you regret and send a message to your subconscious mind that you are unable to complete the targets you give your mind, and it applies the same thought for other things you do in life.

So instead of setting an alarm to wake up early, try going to bed early so you can have a sound sleep and wake up at the right time. That is easily achievable and thus keeps your confidence intact.

These lines by Cynthia Kersey have always hit me hard, and I want to share them with you today,

"Believe in yourself and there will come a day when others will have no choice but to believe with you."

Patience

"Patience is not the ability to wait, but the ability to keep a good attitude while waiting."

- Joyce Meyer

Patience is the power that turns the impossible into possible. Nature itself teaches us to be patient, be it a tiny seed turning into a gigantic tree over time or a mother keeping her baby for 9 months in her womb to finally see a healthy child coming into this world. I have always felt that even though some people by nature are patient, it can be practiced as well.

People often understand patience in the wrong sense. Your situation also has a role to play here. One cannot be patient forever. If you are in a toxic environment, being patient and reaching your threshold won't solve any problem. Say, you are in an abusive relationship, or your partner doesn't reciprocate the love and affection. In this situation, assuming that things will turn well someday will never be helpful. If you have a toxic job where your boss never values your efforts or a toxic business where you are continuously suffering losses, being patient will be of no good here. You will have to come out of these situations and move on.

Accept that the toxic relationship, job, or business is not what you deserve and make a new start. And that's where patience will play its role. When you start a new chapter at any stage of your life, you need to believe that you have taken a step that now requires a bit of a positive attitude and belief in yourself. I always suggest people read the book "Power of Patience" by MJ Ryan.

I too have had a fair share of experience with being patient and not giving up. I was stuck in my CA finals for a long time. I gave my best but still couldn't pass that exam. It had been a difficult one for me, and I decided that I could not waste my entire life cracking an exam and losing my confidence forever. I decided to move on.

Started a company of my own and now it's all going great.

Today I run two companies and an NGO of my own. I learned all throughout that patience plays a large chunk during your journey. Leaving all my efforts behind and choosing a completely different path was not at all an easy choice. It was the scariest, but I always told myself, "Neelam, be patient for a while because everything happens for a reason." You know the mind is the stupidest part of the body. It starts believing what you feed it. So, I kept patience, and I kept moving forward. Keeping in mind what *A.A. Milne said* in *Winnie-the-Pooh*:

"Rivers know this: there is no hurry. We shall get there someday."

Even in small issues in life, like when you are discussing something with your family and an argument starts, and if you do not show patience, things can turn very ugly sometimes.

All in all, you have to keep telling yourself these few things so that you can develop a positive attitude throughout any good or bad situation that needs patience from you.

- Accept that whatever is happening is your reality.
- Keep telling yourself that everything happens for a reason and good things come to those who wait.
- Keep affirming that maybe you do not know why things are happening, but there is some order in this chaos, and one day you will look back and be thankful for all that happened.

Leaving you to sit and reflect on these wonderful lines:

"Patience does not come naturally to anyone; one has to practice it and master it."

ASSOCIATION

"Only these three words decide. Association, Association, Association. Where do you stand today? It's all about your association."

Out of All Seven bridges of success, five bridges of success (Gratitude, Forget the Past, Mindset, Believe in yourself and Patience) that I have talked about in the previous pages, I would say this 6th bridge matters to me the most. I say this because I feel I am the product of all the people I have surrounded myself with in my entire life.

I once read somewhere that you become like the five people you spend the most time with. And I subscribe to this thought that you become the sixth person in that group. Choosing the right people for yourself not only matters the most because they keep you motivated and focused on your goal, but you need those five gems more in the times when you are not at your best.

Suppose you are going through a difficult phase in your life when you have the lowest confidence, you are full of self-doubts, and your self-esteem is going down. What would you need at that moment, the most? I recall these lines by Gift Gugu Mona:

"Dear Daughter,

Choose a good company that will not stain your legacy."

I would want someone who can remind me of my powers and capabilities in the same words as above. Someone who can force me to think in the right and positive direction. That's where the role of the people you associate with comes into play. If your friends, family, or mentors are there for you, then you can overcome any hardship with optimism and strength because you will always have their back.

Stay with people who talk positively to you, support you in your right choices, and guide you in your wrong ones, who are truthful to your face even if it hurts you because they think about your future. Be with people who don't backbite or say ill about you. People who can laugh with you with open hearts and cry with you in your pain are the ones to keep. It's hard to find someone like that, but if you do, stay with them forever.

But sometimes we do not find such people in our lives, and some we can see is mean and selfish people around us who guide us in the wrong way or mislead us. And we know that they are doing so. In that case, just cut off from them and bring something else into your life. Now you will ask, What? I will say, bring five books for yourself. They can be any motivational, philosophical, self-help books, or any book related to your area of interest, by people you love. And today you have social media, go and follow any five people who influence you the most. Watch their lectures or TED talks on YouTube if that guides you toward your purpose and calling.

All in all, you will have to do away with the people who bring your energy down and don't let you be the best version of yourself. I know sometimes it is hard to isolate yourself from that friend you have spent years with or maybe say goodbye to that cousin you have shared laughter with, but once you do it, you will have a new energy flowing into your life, which will give you a sense of positivity, and you will be open to bringing new people who can be your friend, philosopher, and guide for a journey you want to embark on.

If you have big dreams, then you need to make big sacrifices too.

Where do you find yourself standing? In a good company or a bad company?

BAD COMPANY	GOOD COMPANY
Discuss People	Discuss Ideas
Negative approach to life	Positive approach to life
Jealous of others	Support others
Waste time often	Invest time in skills
In their comfort zone	Always pushing their limits
Disrespect others' opinions	Value others' opinions and views
Pessimistic about their future	Optimistic about their future

Opportunity

"If somebody offers you an amazing opportunity but you are not sure you can do it, Say YES then learn how to do it later."

- Richard Branson

Sometimes, we are doing everything right but often neglect the right opportunities that come our way every now and then. We keep on working harder and harder, but we don't always get many opportunities to grow. We have all heard the saying that *opportunity is like ice cream: grab it before it melts.*

I once heard a story in a show with Bill Gates. He was talking about opportunities and how people often say no to them without even thinking once. Bill Gates abruptly says to the interviewer, "I offer you a blank check. You can fill in any amount that you want." The interviewer laughs and says that this interview is not about money, and he can't take the check from him. Bill Gates again invites him to take the check and fill in any amount. But he again says no to it and conveys to him that it's his job to take interviews, and he is not after money. Bill keeps the check inside and then laughs. The interviewer asks him the reason behind his chuckle. He says, "Everybody gets an opportunity in their life, but they don't seize it. You had one to become a billionaire, and you let that opportunity go instead of capturing it. People often do not recognize the opportunities that knock on their door."

If you study the graph of successful people and closely examine it, you will learn that they always seized the opportunities that came their way. And if they did not have any, they created them. Creating an opportunity often involves identifying the situation where you can achieve your goal.

Whenever you see an opportunity coming your way, instead of doubting it and doubting your abilities, think about it. This chance can be a life-changer for you.

Remember that seizing the opportunity not only requires proactive efforts and strategic planning but also a willingness to adapt.

But before you grab an opportunity, prepare your mindset. It will help you understand whether it is the right one for you or not. The right attitude will help you keep your fear of failure aside, and then you can take a calculated risk, which ultimately helps in creating a roadmap to achieve your goals.

Embrace the idea that opportunities are all around you, waiting to be uncovered. All you need is to train your mind so you can see the possibilities that others perceive as obstacles. This mindset shift in your thinking can turn the mundane into extraordinary for you.

The seven bridges of success that I have discussed with you are all equally influential for success. If you look at the most successful people in this world, you will see that they came across all these bridges and crossed each one with patience, resilience, and optimism.

And as Douglas MacArthur said, always remember,

"There is no security on this earth; there is only opportunity."

Part 1

When Puberty Hits

Body Changes

"I love the way I look. I'm fine with it. And if my body changes, I'll be fine with that."

- Gabourey Sidibe

On hitting puberty, we might feel like an ugly duckling. We all did at some point, not because we saw ourselves that way, but most of the time because the people around us made us feel that way.

Some would say, 'Hey! You have so many pimples all over your face,' and many would point out facial hair on boys' faces or the bushy eyebrows of girls. This made us uncomfortable because we were growing taller, according to some people around us. We would then end up bending a little, affecting our posture, and later regretting it.

As teenagers, we've all tried peculiar solutions to our problems and done what we were prohibited from doing. All of this happened because we often didn't communicate our teenage problems with someone who could provide the right solutions. Instead, we discussed them with someone as naïve as we were. Yes, we've all been through this phase during our teenage years.

We often preferred talking to our friends about our problems and tried to avoid our parents as much as we could. I did the same. However, with time, I've realized that parents need to be more open and friendlier with their children at this stage. Children, too, need to understand that parents are the ones who have experienced this before we did and might offer us the best guidance when we're confused about everything happening to us and around us.

Being a girl who has gone through these changes myself, I understand how uncomfortable it feels when you have hair growing on your hands and legs or how shocking and sometimes traumatic it can be when you have your first period. Some don't even understand what is happening to them and cry for hours. This is because we often aren't educated about it beforehand.

Talking about these biological changes used to be a taboo, but that perception is changing today. Even boys, who may not be as open about their emotions as girls, face similar emotional challenges. They might not understand why their voices are changing suddenly and feel awkward about those hints of a beard on their face here and there.

One of the major challenges in this phase is the attraction that boys and girls feel towards each other. Not talking to parents about these changes or parents being immature about them can become a big problem for some during this phase.

Parents need to understand the responsibility of making their kids feel comfortable in their own skin so that these changes don't affect them mentally. Sometimes these developments can scar the child for life, and they can go into complete isolation or a state of hesitation that lasts their entire life.

Both boys and girls should receive equal education about the changes they experience at this age. I've seen boys being insensitive or shy towards girls having their periods in school or in some public place. They try to run from the situation instead of being a bigger person and coming forward to help.

Boys and girls should be educated equally about the menstrual cycle and how it's as natural as breathing. Its significance, even in our Indian culture, should be discussed. Examples of temples like *Kamakhya* in Assam and festivals that celebrate fertility should be explained to children.

Schools also play a crucial role, and parents should ensure that their child's school provides the appropriate sexual education at the right time, without skipping the most important chapter in the biology class. Yes, we all skipped that chapter because our teachers assumed we knew, or maybe they were too shy to discuss it because their teachers also skipped the same chapter.

It's time for parents to stop avoiding those awkward questions. They should understand that the child will seek answers elsewhere, and that place may not be the safest for them.

Children at this age should be politely guided about how sharing with parents or elders, like their siblings, is the best idea because their friends are also going through the same problems and are in the same state of stress and confusion. They may not be the best advisers at this stage of life.

Parents should remember these words of Amy Cuddy while dealing with their adolescents:

"Our bodies change our minds, and our minds can change our behaviour, and our behaviour can change our outcomes."

Body Image

"It doesn't have anything to do with how the world perceives you. What matters is what you see."

Erik Erikson refers to teenagers as the age of Identity Crisis. When we hit puberty, we start becoming conscious of how we look and how others perceive us. We become so fixated on our appearance that we sometimes lose sight of what is truly important at this age—our studies and future career.

One of the most significant changes that occurs in adolescence is the attraction to the opposite sex. Due to a lack of sex education and limited interaction with parents at this age, teenagers may sometimes veer onto the wrong path or even develop unhealthy addictions. Now imagine, at an age when they should be honing their skills and exploring career opportunities, they become ensnared in destructive habits.

I've witnessed teenagers who become so preoccupied with their appearance during this phase that they start losing confidence, becoming introverted, or too shy to speak up. This can have a lasting impact on their overall personality. Some think they're too thin, others too tall, some too short. This is the time when parents should educate them that how they are right now won't define their future, but rather, how they think about themselves and others will. This is when they need their parents the most, yet often receive the least time with them.

Parents play a crucial role here by teaching their children about the importance of health. If they feel they're not in good health, then they need to develop exercise habits or adopt healthier eating habits.

And how could we forget to mention social media? I'm all for it, but only when it's used for the right content, not endless scrolling through reels and shorts for hours on end. Social media has already shortened our attention spans, and we want information in the shortest time possible.

Teenagers are falling into the trap of striving for an 'Instagrammable' life, one that's worthy of posting. To me, all of this seems like a deception. Especially when a teenager is more focused on taking pictures and creating content rather than being enthusiastic about the next book they want to read. It's making our future generation less intellectually engaged and overly reliant on the internet. Moreover, beauty influencers, who are often involved in paid promotions for brands, present an idealized body image to teenagers, intensifying their self-consciousness. I don't want our teenagers emulating beauty influencers at this age. Pursuing six-pack abs, resorting to powders and steroids, or crash dieting and falling ill are not activities suitable for teenagers.

I'm not opposed to looking beautiful or getting healthy, but at this age, when they should be focused on gaining knowledge and building confidence, they're competing to look attractive.

This sets a misguided example of what's truly important—inner beauty or outer beauty. We all know that in the end, inner beauty and mental strength are what truly matter. It's always 'survival of the fittest,' not 'survival of the prettiest.'

DISTRACTIONS

"You can't do big things if you're distracted by small things."

Parties, night outs, travel, alcohol, hangouts, drugs, and whatnot – all of these are the biggest attractions for youngsters, but they are also the biggest distractions.

Teenagers are curious about everything they see around them and want to try things for themselves. When they do so, they are often unaware of the limits they should observe, and that's when they fall into the trap of addiction.

I won't claim that I was never attracted to these fancy things around me. But I soon realized that these things are just a waste of time. I consider myself lucky to have had that realization at the right time. Unfortunately, many children do not receive the right guidance, and they get stuck in a cycle they can't break free from.

I'm not saying that you should embrace complete boredom in your life, but don't make these things your habits and don't prioritize fun and chilling all the time at the expense of your career and education because of a fear of missing out.

Parents have to be extra careful during this phase. It's not the time to be overly strict with your children because the more you shut them out and yell at every little thing, the more they will distance themselves from you. It's a natural tendency for human beings, stemming from the feeling that you no longer accept them as you did when they were kids, running to tell you everything they did during the day at school or with friends.

The bigger problem here is not just that your teenage child is drawn to these addictions, but they also don't share their experiences with you, which closes the door to the right guidance and help.

As a parent, your role is to inform your teenagers at the right time, before they become curious about trying things that may seem cool and Instagram-worthy but could lead them down a dark path.

Always remember that if you don't talk and discuss these matters with your child, someone else surely will, and that someone may not always have their best interests at heart. When teenagers feel unheard at home, they know where they will be heard the most – among their friends and peer groups. What right advice can you expect when the seeker and the adviser are both of the same age group and lack early experience with the situation?

We have a new addiction in the market these days – endless scrolling of social media short videos. You might think that your child isn't prone to addiction while they spend hours consuming shorts and reels in front of you.

Social media certainly has its advantages, but aimless scrolling through videos is a mere waste of time. This calls for a conversation with your child about how they should utilize that time to acquire some skills instead.

And don't assume that your innocent child is immune to pornographic content just because you have parental controls activated on all your subscriptions. After all, social media can easily make such content available to your child without your knowledge.

It might feel like a violation of your teenager's privacy, but if you want to prevent them from falling into the trap of various addictions, it's important to keep your eyes wide open and ears attentive. Always be aware of what your child is drawn to on their phone and always listen to them. You may never understand their inclinations if they start hiding things from you because you didn't take the time to listen and instead resorted to scolding.

Sometimes children fool their parents by pretending to be studying on their phones when they are actually mindlessly scrolling. Parents need to monitor this because it's their duty toward their children, and they shouldn't prioritize privacy over their child's future and mental well-being.

Parents also have another responsibility these days – educating their children about choosing the right partner. Sometimes, teenagers find themselves in toxic relationships without their parents' knowledge. Their behaviour at home may be heavily influenced by this, and it may seem like the child is throwing tantrums when, in reality, your child is in a toxic environment.

Even for teenagers, I have a message: "Focus on your career" is what everyone keeps telling you. And guess what? They're right. Sometimes, we casually dismiss the advice of our elders, but we must be open enough to understand that they have more life experience, even though their lives may have been different. We have more technology at our disposal, but they were teenagers too and experienced similar emotions when they were your age.

We all felt some distance from our parents during our teenage years, often because we weren't ready to talk. If your parent or your elder siblings want to talk, don't shut them down. Have a conversation.

Privacy

When you are distracted by something to which you have become addicted, such as staying up all night chatting with someone, or when you are consumed by social media, spending hours scrolling through it, or when you have become addicted to pornographic content, you stop sharing things with your family because you can't tell them everything that is going on in your life.

Ultimately, whatever you are doing seems wrong at the end of the day, and discussing these things can result in scolding and receiving lengthy lectures about right and wrong.

You start hiding from your family and are always demanding your time, space, and privacy because you feel that your family will not understand what is happening in your life.

Sometimes you do not realize that the path you have taken is not the right one, and you want to pursue it anyhow. That is when you desire the freedom to do anything you like and want to do. When parents impose some restrictions to instill discipline in your life, clashes between the two generations begin.

You must understand that no one is entirely right or wrong here. This is not about who is right and who is wrong. All of this is about what you need to do to make your life right. You have to understand that your parents want the best for you, but in this stage of life, we are always in search of our identity and our place in the society in which we live.

In that search, we are often misdirected or sometimes misguided, which can lead to some difficult moments and situations for us in the present and future, situations that we might end up regretting. So instead, why not understand this beforehand and set your life on the right path from the beginning itself?

Because no one wants to end up as a failure, but some people, addictions, or circumstances can bring setbacks in your life. All I want you to understand at this age is that, instead of asking for privacy and space when you are in your teenage years, you must engage with as many wise people as you can, especially within your family.

I completely understand that some parents are not very friendly, and there may be a communication gap or understanding issues between the teenager and them.

If that is the case with you, you can always rely on an elder sibling or cousin with whom you are comfortable sharing your life. But it should be someone older and wiser in experience than you because someone your age might not provide the best advice, as they may be facing the same issues and might not know what's best to do.

However, someone who is older and has lived through that age and had that sort of experience can better explain what you should do to overcome those distractions.

Here, the parents also play a significant role as they have to understand that their child is going through some changes and is confused about things happening within their mind, body, and outside in the world.

When your child comes and shares their life with you, you must be kind enough to listen and understand their viewpoint instead of being too strict with them. Because if your child feels that you do not understand, they will stop sharing. And that is when you lose them, and misunderstandings develop between the two.

Parents should recall their own time and age. Though things were different in their time, emotions are similar. And there is a high chance that the child might deceive them. But never forget how much you love your child.

REBELLIOUS NATURE

"Children argue because they don't have the right way to make their parents understand them."

Why is everyone always trying to control me? Why does everyone think that I am stupid and immature? What do they want to prove by lecturing me all the time? Why am I always the wrong one in their eyes?

I know these questions have created a cold vibe between you and your family, but you are not alone. Everyone around you has either faced this in their teenage years or is facing it right now. Yes, even your parents have been rebellious on some points with their parents. At least, my parents were, because now they share their stories as they feel it's safe, and I won't be inspired, as I am past that age.

So now you understand why your parents don't share their stories. They don't want to be bad influences on you. They are the well-wishers that God has sent your way in the most natural manner possible.

Friends are an important part of a teenager's life, and they can influence faster than you'd think. Yes, being a parent, you can't simply take away friends who are influencing your child negatively, as that might have the opposite effect. It's always best to talk about what kind of friends your child should make and emphasize the importance of being in good company or no company at all, rather than being in a bad one and potentially ruining their life. Even if you realize late that your teenager is under the wrong influence, it's never too late.

Parents often focus on the fact that their teenager has become rebellious, but they should instead consider why this has happened. There is always a WHY to it. Are they not being heard? Or are they not being understood?

Teenagers often dislike being ordered around, which leads to many fights within the household. The only way to solve this is through communication. Communication is the key that can unlock the door of rebellion and allow your teenager to express the emotions they may be holding against you for whatever reason.

Even teenagers need to understand that arguing all the time with parents or with anyone who criticizes them is not a sign of maturity. In fact, every teenager wants to be seen as a mature adult, so it's important to behave like one until you become one.

You may indeed be misunderstood, but you won't be understood if you stop talking about it. If you are not getting the space and privacy you need, talk about it. If you are comfortable with your mother, tell her. Parents want to listen to you. Sometimes parents lose their temper or make mistakes because they lack understanding about your situation or due to their age and preconceived judgments. This is where you should step in and show them that you are mature enough to discuss it, right?

Parents should acknowledge the effort their child makes in talking to them. They must understand that while their child will always be their child, they are also growing into individuals who go out, experience various things, and get influenced. They are forming their opinions and perceptions based on their experiences in the world at this stage. You are supposed to be their friend, philosopher, and guide, helping them become the best version of themselves.

At this age, try to be less of a parent and more of their friend. Sometimes, when children see other parents being friends with their kids, they wish their parents were like that.

Remember, your child is not a rebel; they are just in a state of chaos, and you are eager to help them through it. Take a step forward and talk to your child, or if you are a teenager reading this, sit down with your mother or father and express how you feel about certain things in life. I bet they are eager to listen to you.

Always remember that no one can replace parents in this world. I'd like to end this chapter by saying something important to children: In the heat of the moment, never say disrespectful things to your parents. They are the ones who care for you the most.

CAREER CONFUSION

When you are in an age group where you are inspired and motivated by every other personality that you see, confusion and a lack of clarity about what you actually want to become are common.

Today, you might see a movie where a police inspector saves people from goons, and you want to be one. But in another moment, you see a politician with power and influence over many, and you might want to be that too.

This leads to more and more confusion about what your real aptitude is and where you can excel. It is always the lack of guidance in the right direction at an early age that causes us to fall into a cocoon of confusion.

We are never told to explore our interests. We are never encouraged to write them down in a notebook and see where we can excel and build a successful career. We are never advised to find that field where we feel no pressure, but instead, we enjoy the activities involved in it.

Instead, many of us find ourselves in situations where we choose streams and careers under the pressure of our family, relatives, or society. But it is always better to realize at an early age where your interests lie and to follow your dreams, rather than spending your crucial years under pressure and ending up with regrets.

When it comes to pursuing our dreams, we often fear that our parents won't understand us. But have you tried? If you truly want to pursue something, then convincing your parents and showing them that you can make a better living out of it is the first step on your path to success.

Zakir Khan, an Indian Standup Comedian, once said beautiful lines in an interview where he stated that your parents are not against your dreams; they just don't want you to be poor.

Even if you have to try and choose something else in your career, never shy away from experimenting and finding your true calling. The more you experiment, fail, and lose interest in something, the closer you get to your true dream—something that you would love to do for the rest of your life, or for a while, without any regrets.

Sometimes, we find ourselves in a job because we had to, maybe due to our financial conditions or other circumstances. However, it's never too late to discover your true purpose, and it's never too difficult to pursue what you love.

If you need to switch your job or change your interests at any point in time, do it. If you cannot leave your current job or field but have always wanted to do something else in life, find just 2 hours from your day for what you love and what makes you happy. You may need to cut some hours from social media or stop scrolling through never-ending reels, but the change you will see in your life in the coming years will be worth it. Who knows, you might even build an amazing career out of your interest and leave behind your current job or the stream you chose under pressure.

Sometimes, we are advised to pursue a certain course but are never guided on how to build a successful career in it or how to approach a job in that field once it is completed. The next step is unclear, and at that moment, you should either take aptitude tests or assess where you currently stand to gain a clear idea of what to do next.

This advice applies even to students who put too much emphasis on a single exam and find themselves in a cycle of failed attempts. Sometimes, they lose their self-confidence and become demotivated to the point of falling into depression. Some students even take drastic measures, which is tragic for society as a whole.

Always remember that nothing is insurmountable. Life was not a bed of roses for anyone, especially for people who have achieved great things. They, too, had their share of struggles, so why fear your own challenges? There is nothing you cannot overcome.

You can always make a fresh start. Don't devote your entire life to an exam or a course that no longer motivates you. The exam is just a part of your life, not your entire life. Set a deadline for yourself, and if you can achieve your goals within that timeframe, go for it. Otherwise, accept your present and make a change. When nothing seems right, it's time to make a change. That's your hint.

Tips you can use to find your true calling:

- Break free from the shackles of your comfort zone. You were not born to stay in your comfort zone for your entire life; you are meant to struggle and achieve.

- Develop self-awareness about your thoughts and desires. Listen to your heart's true desires by sitting in silence and understanding what you really want.
- Take a pen and paper and write down your thoughts, desires, aims, and life goals. Writing will help you solidify your calling.
- Begin developing skills in the areas that interest you the most. Start slowly if you can't dedicate much time right now.
- Share your aspirations with the right people who will listen and support you in pursuing your calling.

How can you convince your parents to support your dreams?

- Stay as calm as possible when discussing your dreams with your parents. They want to listen, but your manner and tone can affect their response.
- If someone in your family can influence your parents, reach out to them first and ask for their support in conveying your dreams.
- Actions speak louder than words. Demonstrate through your actions that your dreams truly matter to you and that you are willing to put in all your effort to achieve them.
- Provide them with an alternative plan in case your initial plan doesn't succeed. They are often more concerned about failure than success and don't want to see you fail.

IDENTITY CRISIS

Erik Erikson refers to the teenage years as an age of Identity Crisis.

It is true that as teenagers, we are always searching for our place in the family, among friends, and in society. We are in search of our purpose. We question ourselves and the people around us. Yes, it happens to everyone. You are not alone in this. We feel that everyone is taking us for granted all the time, and we want to be valued by the people around us. This is the age when we are in search of our own identity and place in this world.

But this is also the age when we are not completely mature yet not completely immature. Our parents assume us to be young in age and experience, but we see ourselves growing. There is a conflict about everything around us. Youngsters even seclude themselves when they are not given the preference and involvement they need during this time.

The generation gap plays a role here. Youngsters want to express their opinions about things, but parents don't want that because, for them, their children are still too young to speak about adult issues. However, the opportunity to be the bigger person here lies with the parents. They must understand that their child is going through a phase where they want a place and a voice among their peers, and if they are shut in their own house with immaturity, they will cut themselves off, and that won't be good for anyone. Parents must remain calm and explain to their teenagers in a poised manner the differences in views that occur instead of starting an argument with them. This is the age of storms for teenagers, and those storms can become havoc if preparations are not made right.

At this age, when teenagers idolize teachers or celebrities from around the world, they try to be exactly like them, not an inch different, and they want it to be perfect. Although the real world around them can be different, they won't understand it until they experience it themselves.

To help shape them into your version of perfect, parents need to recognize the fact that their child is in a stage where they are discovering many new thoughts in the world, and many new "-isms" are being explained to them in their social science class. Sometimes, they would like to bring some change to the world around them, and as their teachers told them, that change should start at home itself.

Teenagers often engage in controversies with their parents over their ideas and opinions about the issues happening in the world. Parents might have one opinion, and the child may have a completely different one. In that case, the best approach is to let your child know the other perspective. Instead of turning it into a never-ending argument, leave it to their judgment after making them aware of the other side. This will help both parents and the child avoid making things ugly between them.

This advice is also for the children because everyone at this age goes into an illusion that they are the only ones who are right in the room, and the rest of the people are old and know nothing about the modern world. But this is not true; children cannot compete with the years of experience that parents and elders have.

So, be patient and always lend an ear to what your parents have to say. Even if you do not agree, it's never wrong to listen to the other side. That's the first step towards maturity.

How can parents help their child navigate the identity crisis stage?

- Encourage your children to read books or watch movies and documentaries that can help them understand the diversity that exists.
- Also, at this age, encourage your child to interact with people of different identities.
- If your child needs therapy at any stage, don't hesitate to seek it. Identity crisis is not a mental health issue, but the child may struggle emotionally and mentally during this period.
- As their loved ones, support them in their journey of self-discovery in the changing world around them

Self-Doubt

"If you hear a voice within you say 'you cannot paint,' then by all means paint, and that voice will be silenced."

- Vincent Willem van Gogh

As a teenager, we often grapple with numerous doubts – doubts about our looks, talents, and capabilities, among other things. These doubts arise because we lack confidence due to a lack of knowledge and experience. If we do not address these doubts early on, they can become deeply ingrained within us for an extended period. Doubts hinder our ability to dream big and can lead to prolonged contemplation, preventing us from making significant life-changing decisions. This is especially true when it comes to choosing our career paths, considering changes in our fields of study, or making personal decisions about relationships and marriage.

However, having faith in ourselves and our decisions is the greatest strength we can possess, ultimately contributing to success in life. We should make informed decisions based on proper and sufficient knowledge, either from experts or individuals with relevant experiences. Once we commit to a decision, we must approach it with unwavering self-belief and train our minds to take full responsibility for the outcomes. Taking responsibility not only prepares us for the next steps or endeavors but also boosts our confidence, preventing us from falling into the trap of self-doubt. Instead, it fosters courage and optimism, empowering us to move forward and learn from past mistakes.

Additionally, we should refrain from comparing ourselves to others, as this can breed self-doubt and hinder personal growth. Instead, we should invest our time and effort in self-improvement, honing our skills and talents. While our qualities may not align with those of the people we admire, this does not mean we lack unique and exceptional qualities within ourselves. There may be aspects hidden within us that are absent in the individuals we aspire to become.

Even the Bhagavad Gita emphasizes that a person who doubts themselves cannot attain success. To overcome the clutches of self-doubt, we must seek knowledge and dispel all fears about ourselves.

Now, the pressing question is where to acquire this knowledge. We have access to books, parental guidance, insights from elders, and, in today's digital age, social media experts and YouTube channels that offer valuable assistance. To succeed, we need to maintain unwavering focus on our goals and resist distractions, a discipline that demands considerable effort.

We are familiar with the story of Hanuman from the Ramayana, who was renowned for his strength, knowledge, and wisdom. However, there was a point in his life when he had forgotten about his inherent strengths and capabilities.

He needed a mentor to remind him of his hidden potential, and once he regained confidence in himself, there was no turning back for Hanuman.

So, when overwhelmed by self-doubt, all we need to do is awaken the hidden Hanuman within us, recall our strengths, and believe in ourselves. We can conquer the world and should never allow anyone to sow the seeds of self-doubt within us.

PEER GROUP

"Always surround yourself with people who lift you up, rather than hold you down."

- Donald L. Hicks, Look into the stillness

Your peer group shapes your associations. The company you keep is a crucial factor in every stage of life. It's often said that you become a product of the five people you spend the most time with. Having the right associates is especially vital during your teenage years as it significantly influences your thought formation and your attitude toward life. It has a long-lasting impact on you, which is why being in the right company is essential for your personal growth.

When people claim that they are not in bad company and have benefited from it in life, they may overlook the advantages they could have gained by associating with individuals who could have brought positive changes into their lives. While it's important to avoid negative associations, we sometimes neglect the importance of seeking out positive company. The more time we spend with individuals who prioritize growth and positivity in life, the more positive changes we will introduce into our own lives.

This is an age when we connect with our emotions more deeply, making it crucial for us to be discerning about our associations. Sometimes, we become entangled with the wrong people, and before we realize it, it becomes too late, or we have wasted a significant amount of our precious time engaging with them. Time is valuable, so always spend it with the right people who help you become a better version of yourself, rather than being with those who bring you down or add no value to your life.

The interests that endure throughout your life are often developed during your teenage years and are heavily influenced by the people you associate with. For instance, consider a child who loves spending time with friends who read and share their reading experiences, and another child who spends time with a peer group that engages in constant gossip and discussion about others. Who do you think will learn more? Now, put yourself in a similar situation and think about the company you would choose for yourself.

If, while reading this, you feel that you have been in the wrong company for a long time and have no idea how to leave that peer group, just consider one thing: what is more important, your life or being among those so-called "cool" people who hinder your growth and learning? You have to make a choice, always. If you choose yourself over the wrong peer group, you have leveled up. If you can't cut ties all at once, start by avoiding and talking less with them initially. Gradually and steadily, remove all toxic associations that hinder your success in life. This is an age that determines your future, and you undoubtedly want it to be bright. So, to have a bright future, you must choose your companions wisely.

I have witnessed teenagers who become entangled with the wrong peer group and end up taking destructive paths in life. They become addicted to drugs, alcohol, theft, and other harmful habits that can ruin their lives. Before you fall into this trap, set your life ideals. To be valued among people, you must have values in life and boundaries that you set for yourself. No one should be able to push you beyond these boundaries; that should be your strength.

Once you do that, you will notice that people recognize you for who you are. For example, if you are deeply committed to your studies and believe that skipping classes is not a good idea, make it clear to your friends by not joining them in skipping classes and establishing your ideals from the outset. Some may not accept you because they consider you "uncool," but that's what sets you apart. You should embrace that about yourself—the uniqueness you attain because of the company you keep. Everyone has their definition of fun; perhaps, traveling is fun for you, while solitude is enjoyable for someone else. Decide what's fun for you and stick to it; don't change your true nature for others but only for yourself.

It can be challenging to be different from the majority, but you will always find people who appreciate you for who you are. Whatever you do, do it with joy, and don't allow any habit or person to become your addiction. As one of my friends once said, it's okay to be alone rather than be with someone who leaves a negative impact on your life and stains your memories forever.

Money Through Shortcut

"If you take shortcuts, you get cut short."

- Gary Busey

Teenage is an age where you tend to identify and relate more with your peers than anything else. However, it's common knowledge that your associations can either build you up or break you down. Emotions play a significant role during this phase, making it crucial to choose our social circles carefully, as they define our present and shape our future selves.

When you form good and healthy associations at an early age, not only do you grow, but your peers grow with you. These associations stay with you for a lifetime, as they influenced you during the formative years when you were shaping your entire personality.

However, some teenagers fall into associations that are not just wrong in terms of their thought processes and attitudes toward life, but also engage in mischievous and even illegal activities that can have life-altering consequences.

I've come across newspaper articles discussing how today's youth can fall into the trap of seeking shortcuts to make money quickly, resorting to illegal activities that can lead them into a life of crime and imprisonment. Some are driven by family circumstances, while others seek to fulfill their desires, often resorting to illicit means.

Instances have occurred where individuals borrowed money from friends, placed it all on bets, lost it, and subsequently found themselves in violent altercations. All of this stemmed from initially associating with the wrong crowd. Given that children may not be fully aware at this age, the onus lies on elders to prevent them from getting entangled in such situations.

With the advent of social media, falling into debt traps and gambling has become easier. This places an even greater responsibility on parents to keep a watchful eye on teenagers and engage in open communication about the potential harm these activities can cause to their lives.

I've encountered applications that offer easy loans to students, only to exploit them when they're unable to repay the exorbitant interest rates. These unscrupulous entities resort to blackmail, threatening to leak compromising photos to their contacts. It's imperative that students are educated about these scams, and that strict government regulations are implemented to counter such practices. Until then, it is our shared responsibility to ensure that our innocent children do not fall victim to them.

While betting apps may seem like a convenient way to make some quick cash, it's crucial to pay heed to the rapid warnings about their addictive nature. When even the creators of these applications issue such warnings, it's a clear signal that caution should be exercised. We all know that everything that appears trendy holds the most allure at this age. You're not alone; every person has faced similar temptations. Some chose the right path, while others veered off course. The choice now lies with you.

I have one resounding message: this age is when your interests are shaped, interests that you'll carry forward. If you choose negative influences now, you'll carry them into your future, potentially leading to a troubled life. Avoid falling into the false belief that money is the sole source of happiness, or that the sole purpose in life is to amass wealth.

While achieving financial success should be a goal, it should not be the sole aim in life. Recognizing this in your teenage years will be a source of gratitude in the future. If you fail to realize it now, life will likely teach you later – it does so for everyone. Ultimately, what matters most is being able to look at yourself in the mirror each day.

Always bear in mind the words of Tomas Gavlas:

"Don't take shortcuts to gain small profits which don't lead to great things, but stay true to your guiding intent."

Part 2

Work Hard & Chill

Health is Wealth

"Take care of your body. It's the only place you have to live."

- Jim Rohn

Suppose God came and offered you the wealth of the entire world, but you couldn't move and were bedridden for your entire life, or you could have a healthy body, mind, and soul but would have to earn everything else yourself. What would you wish for? I know what your answer would be: a healthy body, mind, and soul. What's the use of wealth if you're not fit and healthy enough to enjoy it and experience the happiness it brings?

Good health is as essential as breathing. An unhealthy lifestyle has become so common that we often don't realize we've been sitting at our laptops for continuous eight hours. And what do we expect from our bodies, which were designed for physical activity? This sedentary lifestyle is becoming a curse in our society. We spend our entire lives earning wealth, often neglecting our health, and when it's time to enjoy that wealth, we find ourselves in a hospital bed, spending our hard-earned money on healthcare. What irony!

There was a time when I used to hear grandparents talk about their joint pains, neck aches, and backaches, but now I see more young people complaining about these issues. The reason is simple: people used to experience these problems in their later years due to aging when they were physically active. However, due to the absence of yoga or regular exercise in people's lives today, these ailments are afflicting them at a young age, reducing their life expectancy. According to numerous studies, mortality rates are rising faster among younger people than older ones.

We've been neglecting our health, our greatest wealth, and only realize its value when it's lost. We've been eating pizza nonstop to cope with stress, binge-watching and binge-eating for hours when we're depressed. Have we not? Can we control it? If not, who will? No one will get you out of bed and help you shed that excess weight. We all love the lifestyle of metro cities, but in reality, these cities are leading us towards a sedentary lifestyle dominated by office work, laptops, and mobile phones, with minimal physical activity. The end result is a body riddled with diseases.

I understand that you have a 9-to-5 job, and I'm not suggesting you abandon your work and become a hermit doing yoga in the Himalayas. However, you can at least dedicate a 30-minute session to yoga or another form of exercise to maintain long-term fitness. Nothing more, nothing less. You'll notice changes even in your decision-making once you become healthy.

Instead, what we often do is get highly motivated one day after seeing a social media reel showcasing a transformation journey. We put on our running shoes, engage in half an hour of intense exercise, and end up exhausted with sore muscles that discourage us from getting up the next day. Believe me, this is the primary reason why you give up on your quest for good health, and it turns out to be a major mistake.

Always remember that your goal should be a healthy body, a healthy mind, and a healthy soul, not just six-pack abs or a slim figure. I know it's challenging to start this lifestyle shift, but you need to be mentally strong with a positive mindset. Getting influenced by a 60-second video on social media won't be enough. It's better to initiate this change on your own rather than being forced into it by doctors after you fall ill.

The key mantra to start is to "START SLOW." Don't rush into intense exercise or sign up for a gym membership just to achieve a perfect physique. Begin slowly at your own pace. Watch some YouTube videos and start with simple yoga poses. Build up a routine, dedicating 15 minutes daily, and gradually increase your time as you become more comfortable. Go for brisk walks in the morning, drink at least 5 to 6 glasses of water (instead of 8), and eat some fruit every day. For instance, make your fruit consumption visually appealing by cutting them in an attractive manner. This is a tried and tested method.

I used to be the laziest person when it came to exercising, but starting slowly and gradually building a routine has made me feel better, and I continue to exercise for my own health.

Always remember, "*Healing your body, mind, and soul will automatically heal everything in your life.*"

HEALTHY MIND

"No food will ever hurt you as much as an unhealthy mind"

- Brittany Burgunder

I have seen many individuals with amazing bodies and high fitness levels giving up on life. I have witnessed elderly people ending their lives even after enduring all the challenges life threw their way.

I have even observed officers and people in respected positions with significant social responsibilities, who had successfully cleared major exams like UPSC, resorting to suicide due to family or relationship issues. I understand that one might argue it's easy to comment unless you've been in their shoes, but what is the root of the problem here? What takes precedence over one's life? What seems easier than facing life itself?

I would say, the mind. To put it plainly, they were mentally weak. The mind is the culprit, but it can also be the savior if we control it instead of letting it control us. A healthy mind is as important as a healthy body.

We have always prioritized a healthy body over a healthy mind. We often hear the saying, "A sound mind in a sound body." But do you know why some people are more successful than others, or why some take longer to achieve similar goals?

The key difference lies in the state of their minds. And when I talk about the mind, I'm not referring to intelligence, but rather the state of your mind and your thought process. A healthy mind is more focused, able to discern situations easily, and find solutions to them.

Your mind will process whatever you feed it. Fill it with negative emotions and thoughts, and you may spiral into depression. However, start feeding it positive thoughts and watch yourself shine. In other words, the mind can be easily influenced.

However, our minds don't operate in isolation. They are influenced by the activities we engage in and the people we associate with.

If you want a peaceful mind, distance yourself from negative people. That's the first step you can take immediately for your mental peace. But after that, you'll need some detoxification for a healthy mind—a clean slate after years of accumulation.

Start with forgiveness and utter the words *'I forgive you'* frequently. You can do this when you take responsibility for your own actions. Learn from your past and let go. Don't hold onto it, as it will only stagnate your life.

Focus on the present moment, even though it's challenging because, as human beings, we seek the safety of our comfort zones. But once you practice this, life will be mentally easier.

Get involved socially, without any ulterior motives, and help people. Engage in activities you love. If you enjoy reading, pick up a book. I'd recommend *'Energize Your Mind' by Gaur Gopal Das.* If gardening is your thing, start with a small indoor plant on your desk. If you enjoy playing, solve puzzles or play with your loved ones. It'll transport you back to the peacefulness of your childhood.

Some people thrive on challenges to stimulate their neurons. If you have no one to challenge, challenge yourself. If you're right-handed, challenge yourself to write the alphabet with your left hand.

Some individuals are naturally sociable. Meet with people often, if it brings you inner peace and maintains your sanity. You can even practice affirmations if you resonate with the concept. It's a good way to convince your mind that *"All is well,"* as the movie '3 Idiots' emphasized.

What I want to convey through this chapter to your mind is, stay well! And to you, I want to express that if you have a sane mind that isn't overburdened with excessive thoughts, consider yourself blessed. This universe is ready to grant you whatever you desire, but it ensures you're mentally prepared for it.

If you possess a mind that isn't delving too deeply into a whirlpool of thoughts, be grateful for it, especially in this age of social media where many minds are troubled simply because they saw friends enjoying themselves and are now experiencing FOMO.

As someone once said, happiness is overrated. So, don't let your mind deceive you into thinking you're not as happy as others, because if it's doing that, BEEP BEEP ! It's an alarm for you to embark on a mind detox.

And if you're feeling too overwhelmed to start right now, I'd suggest something in line with Lailah Gifty Akita's words from 'Pearls of Wisdom', which I follow when my mind attempts to overwhelm me:

"Worry less, pray more."

HEALTHY SOUL

"Show me the most damaged part of your soul, and I will show you how it still shines like Gold."

- Nikita Gill

Usually, when we talk about the soul, we think we have to be spiritual even though we are not inclined towards it. Some even think that talking about souls is an old person's deed, and young people don't have to care about such deep things in life at such an early age.

But what if I tell you that caring and connecting with your soul can help you achieve more in life, be it name, fame, money, or success in any field? This may sound like something funny and out of your league, but it is an actual proven theory. In other words, it's like a miracle that can happen in your life. However, what matters most here is trust—trusting in what you believe in, and change in your life will become inevitable.

I have seen many experiences of this, including my own. You will even get more than what you have wished for if you start connecting with your soul. I know not everyone reading this would be able to relate to what I am saying, and not everyone will be interested in knowing about it, but if I say so, it may hurt a little that not everyone experiences miracles in their life.

Most people come and go without making much of an impact in their own lives or the lives of other people. But I am sure that if you have chosen to read this book, then you are someone who wants to achieve something significant and make something big of yourself.

Enough of talking now because one could write a complete book on the soul and its nature. In this chapter, we will only explore how you can keep a healthy soul. Sometimes, we often hear about something too often but are never able to understand its importance. There is one such technique that can make your soul healthy, and you all know it but have never tried it.

Believe me, it's not easy to start, but once you master it, you will never stop. The one-word solution for a healthy soul is MEDITATION. Yes! We often hear about mindfulness, as the new-age people call it. Thanks to Adiyogi and our ancient Indian Yogis who have proven time and again how meditation can change a person's journey.

It's hard to meditate in the beginning, but that's the only tricky part. Start slowly, as I always say. Begin with just five minutes a day. You can start with a short Pranayam session. Visualize success, happiness, or whatever goals you have. Choose a quiet place where no one disturbs you. It's just you and your solitude. Sit with yourself. Experience the joy in your mind. Visualize and feel how you will feel once you achieve your goals.

It works when you create the same circumstances in your mind as you would feel on the day you have conquered your goals. Once you start enjoying it, increase the duration of your meditation sessions.

Once you start practicing meditation daily (which is an achievement in itself when done consistently), miracles will unfold. You will become more positive and patient with yourself and others around you. Of course, you will have to deal with negative emotions and thoughts while meditating but let them come and go. Focus on your visualization. Also, try to discover your soul's purpose by asking yourself that question. You may even find answers in nature's unique ways. You can even find solutions to your life problems while meditating on them.

For those who find meditation difficult, there's another way to keep your soul healthy and full. Spend time in nature, feeding birds and animals around you. It fills your heart with contentment. You must have done it at some point in time. Remember how relaxed it felt? Why not do it more often?

I also feel my soul laugh when I am sitting with my loved ones, sharing hearty laughs with them. So, laugh as much as you can and make others laugh too. A healthy soul will automatically connect you to yourself and your purpose. For a healthy soul, you will also need a healthy mind, which I will discuss in the coming chapter.

But from now on, always remember:

"A healthy soul always has a kind heart, a peaceful mind, and a loving nature, where others feel safe and blissful."

Career Settlement

"Even though your time on the job is temporary, if you do a good enough job, your work there will last forever."

- Idowu Koyenikan, Wealth for All

If you are in your 30s and still confused about your actual career or are not yet settled in your life, if wherever you are right now doesn't feel like the right place, and you feel like a square peg in a round hole, then you surely need to read this chapter. Let's talk about taking an interest in what you do. Many people face this issue: they don't like what they are doing or they liked it at one point in time but now they don't.

I believe that enjoying what you do is important if you want something big out of it. If you have limitations in life, then progress becomes slow. And if you are not enjoying what you do, then maybe it's high time that you sit down and take time to think about your career path.

I understand that some people are bound by responsibilities and can't take risks in life, or they have a family to take care of and bills to pay. But if you can, then think of it this way: what if you were told to marry somebody? Would you just go ahead and marry them? Of course not. You would take time to get to know that person, to understand if you both are compatible, right?

When you choose a career, it's exactly like getting into a relationship. You will be in a relationship with your career for another 25 to 30 years. That's why I say, be in a career you love, just like they say, marry someone you love. And believe me, you will enjoy and start living life to the fullest.

So, what is the actual way to settle into a career you love? Wherever you are, just pause for a moment. Take some time for yourself and think. You have to self-analyze and self-reflect. And during this entire time, you will have to make a promise to be truthful to yourself. And remember, it's never too late to make a career change. Everyone has their time, and yours is yet to come.

In management, there is a technique I learned in college called SWOT Analysis. Take a diary and write down your strengths (S), weaknesses (W), opportunities (O), and threats or risks (T). Once you have done that, you will know more about yourself and what you are good at. This will bring you closer to a clear understanding of your passions. Recognizing what you are passionate about and identifying your strengths will be your first step toward achieving your dream career, which is the most challenging part of all the steps.

A clear understanding is a step towards better action because 90% of people don't know their strengths and stumble at this very step. They are never able to break free from the cycle of disliking the jobs they are doing. Whatever action plan you make, take it slow.

Even though you may have big dreams, putting all your resources in at once is never a good idea. Create action plans for slow and steady steps. For example, if you are currently working in a software company but dream of pursuing a music career when you are 50, that is where you see yourself in the future. Start with a YouTube channel instead of releasing an album without any audience and investing all your hard-earned money at once.

Or if you are in the human resource department of your company but aspire to grow in the marketing department, invest in your skills, learn marketing slowly, build your strengths over time, and address your weaknesses and threats. When the opportunity is right, take the big leap of your life and start applying with confidence. Investing in your skills will be the biggest investment for your future success.

You will have to remember one thing throughout the process: trust the process. Even if you are dedicating just 15 minutes to your dream job, give those 15 minutes daily without thinking twice about what the result will be. This concept is akin to 'Nishkam Karm,' which Krishna explains to Arjuna in the Bhagavad Gita.

Usually, when we are uncertain about our interests and what we truly want to do, we engage in multiple activities and keep ourselves so busy that we can't focus on our true potential. Instead, pick one area and master it.

Some steps might seem too easy or idealistic, but that's how it works. When you start working on something of your own, say you want to set up a business and envision yourself as an entrepreneur of the future, work on building your professional network in your business field.

Ensure that your ideas have the potential to support your financial needs. And when your business idea starts working, focus on technology updates, financial planning, customer satisfaction, and repeat orders to help it grow. You can also work on creating multiple income sources.

Once you start making profits, reinvest that money in marketing and advertisement to expand your business. Try to generate excitement among people for whatever you do. This works best when you have a large audience to serve. Utilize online platforms for this purpose because they have a vast audience.

Always remember that while you are working toward your dream job, never compromise your health and family. Work-life balance is essential for maintaining your mental sanity in this competitive world.

I am not saying that you will never experience failures in life. That's impossible; everyone does. But what you need to focus on is not accepting failure. An entrepreneurial mindset will help you here because an employee mindset can lead to failure when you are working on your own idea. I would suggest reading the book '*Cash Flow Quadrant*' for more on this topic.

However, executing things in a systematic order will surely expedite your journey. Working systematically is crucial because I have seen people with great ideas for businesses but never working on those ideas, leading to failure.

Take things one step at a time, work on all areas slowly and steadily, and you will not even realize how easy it was. It will all seem like a dream, just as it does to me today.

I don't even feel that I have built for myself what I always wanted. But I kept the faith and worked on it. Life is not a blockbuster movie; there is no one big shot. Come back to reality, get up, and work for yourself. I may sound harsh, but the truth is that you alone can change your life, and that's only when you truly and desperately want to. *Intention always matters in your journey to success.*

I know some people are content in their 9-to-5 jobs and cherish the stability they have in life. But if they have desires to do something else, then they should definitely work on it.

When you have decided that you are ready to take the career leap for yourself, always remember:

"True career fulfillment is achieved when your passion for your work aligns harmoniously with your sense of purpose in life."

LOVE

"The meeting of two personalities is like the contact of two chemical substances: if there is any reaction, both are transformed."

- Carl Gustav Jung

Loving someone is easy, but love is complicated because everyone has their own definition of love. For you, what you have may be love, but the other person may not perceive it the same way. It becomes even more important to discuss love because I have seen many of my friends jeopardizing their careers and youth for people they believed they loved, but it wasn't reciprocated. Not only did their careers suffer, but they also experienced emotional, mental, and physical distress.

Today's youth is more open about love and being in relationships. Many are in open relationships, while some are in hidden ones. But the point here is, are we, as millennials, experiencing true love? Do we understand what love is? And are we investing our time in the right places?

I have always relied on four pillars to determine if any relationship I had was worth investing my time and feelings in: Loyalty, Respect, Trust, and Communication. I consider transparency to be the foundation of any relationship, as it creates a safe space where thoughts can be shared and feelings can be expressed without fear of judgment.

But before delving into any relationship talk, let's explore whether being in a relationship is worth it or not. What is more important, career or relationship? Does being in a relationship hinder your career?

We know that emotions play a significant role in any relationship because we are affected through emotions alone. But we should not forget the person we are in a relationship with. They are affected too. So, if you are serious about someone and can envision taking it to the next level, then only invest your time and effort in it; otherwise, you will end up hurting yourself and the other person.

Sometimes, people are never able to move on. They even compromise their careers for the wrong person. I always suggest working on the four pillars to determine if what you are feeling is love and not mere physical attraction.

Once you start feeling a connection because you have shared your ambitions, dreams, future goals, achievements, strengths, and weaknesses, and the other person is on the same page as you, consider taking the relationship to the next level.

When you do so, honesty plays the most significant role in strengthening your love. Every two individuals will have differences of opinion. If things take an ugly turn during discussions, practice silence for the time being. When both of you are calm, then address the matter and communicate your points to resolve the issues. Remember that a relationship involves two people, so effort should always come from both sides; otherwise, you will lose your self-worth and, consequently, your self-esteem.

These pointers apply to normal relationships, but if you find yourself in an unhealthy relationship where your partner tries to gaslight, exhibits narcissistic behaviour, or abuses you in any form, that is non-negotiable.

Recognizing if you are in a toxic relationship is as crucial as feeling love in any relationship. Every toxic relationship exhibits symptoms. Detecting them and standing up for yourself is not only important for your future but also for your overall well-being.

If your partner is constantly criticizing you, blaming you for everything wrong, trying to belittle you, always finding faults, abusing you, harassing you publicly, and never apologizing for their bad behaviour, then your alarms should definitely go off.

You need to talk to them about it and take some time off to understand the other person's intentions. And if it is just you who is suffering more, then choosing yourself and your happiness will never be considered selfish on your part. Believe me, if God were allowed to decide, you would be chosen first.

If your partner is abusive and is tormenting you mentally, emotionally, and physically, then the safest option is always to share it with someone close and keep them informed. Seek help to exit this relationship before it destroys your existence and takes away your life. Nothing is more precious than that.

Be courageous, be self-aware, and decide to MOVE OUT ASAP! When in doubt, choose your personal growth, self-love, and healing over anything else. True love never makes you suffer or hinders your path; instead, it paves the way for your growth and development.

However, when you come out of a relationship, moving on with your life and healing can be difficult. But have patience, dedicate time to yourself, exercise, meditate, read, do what you like, and prioritize yourself. Regain your self-worth and never forget that you haven't lost all the love. Just look at your parents. Nothing can be purer than a parent's love.

There have been cases, especially in our country, where two people had to separate because their parents were against their relationship for various reasons.

I have always felt that parents never think ill of their children. However, some parents may have a certain mindset shaped by their upbringing, and those thoughts cannot be changed overnight. If you feel that your partner is the one, then be patient enough to wait for them and make your parents understand your true love.

Never rush because it shows your eagerness to be with the other person, indicating your immaturity about your relationship, and that you are willing to compromise your relationship with your parents. If your partner loves you, they will understand and wait for you. And if not, then maybe you should reconsider.

Never disrespect or hurt your parents to start a relationship. I believe that parents should become more open-minded and give their children a chance, trying to understand their love if their child has chosen someone they would have chosen. Because:

"Love is a beautiful journey that requires your investment in the form of time and support, building an empire where the joy of a successful and happy marriage resides."

Marriage

"A great marriage is not when the 'perfect couple' comes together. It is when an imperfect couple learns to enjoy their differences."

- Dave Meurer

When I discuss marriage, and as you read about it, we are on the same page regarding the need for stability in life. Marriage, in itself, is a symbol of stability.

For me, marriage has never been merely a union of two people, as we have often seen depicted in TV serials and Bollywood movies. Especially in India, where family forms the foundation of society, marriage is a union of two families.

While some may view marriage as a hindrance in their life, I hold a different perspective. I consider marriage a catalyst in one's life, but only if you can find the right partner who seamlessly fits into your life, much like a jigsaw puzzle.

For me, the primary reason to marry someone should be love, and nothing else. Marriage should not be driven by financial considerations or physical attributes but by the person themselves. When we talk about the person, we refer to their personality and the vibe they exude. If their frequency aligns with yours, and you both connect on a deep level, then marriage is worth considering. Finding the right life partner feels like heaven, while ending up with the wrong one can feel like living in hell.

When I think about the perfect partner and a happy marriage, although there's no universal definition, I find two things to be paramount: the relationship you share with your partner and the relationship both of you have with each other's families. If either of these aspects is affected, the likelihood of conflicts in the marriage increases.

I always say, "Marriage is like a newborn baby; it requires trust, attention, love, and care."

First, let's discuss strengthening your relationship with your partner, as this will ultimately lead to fewer conflicts with the family as well. The couple needs to set some ground rules in their relationship because they will help you resolve your differences faster than ever. On top should be to not sleep until you resolve your issues and give each other a goodnight kiss.

Sometimes, in the heat of the moment or in a bid to prove your point right, either of the partners can prolong the fight. Instead, you should try to stop the fight mid-way until the other partner is cool-headed. Take up the issue when the heat between the two is gone. And never ever leave for your office or anywhere you go without a warm hug. This makes your love stronger each day.

I have seen some couples have the habit of airing their dirty laundry in public. Discussing your private life with others can belittle your relationship with your partner.

This is not advisable for toxic or abusive relationships. Some things are non-negotiable, and firstly talking to your partner about it is crucial.

I have seen that some people even have jealousy, self-pride, or ego in their relationship, which is one of the reasons for conflicts in marriage and breakups in any relationship. They should never come in between; instead, they should be replaced with compliments and praise for each other's qualities and achievements. Even if your partner has habits that you don't like, talking is the only solution to any issue. If they are wise, they will surely listen and understand your concern.

I think that when we don't share our loving private moments with anyone, then why share little arguments that only we can solve, and no other third person?

Because talking about your partner's weaknesses publicly or criticizing them in front of others will only lead to a bitter feeling between you two. I could go on and on talking about men and women in a marriage, but I would surely recommend reading an entire book written on this topic called 'Men Are from Mars; Women Are from Venus' by John Gray.

Now, let us talk about how you can form a cordial bond with your partner's family. Here, I would like to put special emphasis on girls because a major part of their life changes when they leave their parents' house and move into a new family for the rest of their lives. I feel that in this context, women bear a greater responsibility because they have to adapt to a new family.

The easiest way to do it is to accept the family wholeheartedly. Just think of it this way: the love between you and your partner is only possible because of the man and woman behind your partner's birth. Loving them should be a natural outcome, and it's a beautiful thing.

I feel the biggest problem arises when girls who have lived in a completely different culture and atmosphere have to adapt to a new one. Out of human nature, they may want to change the rituals to match their own upbringing. Girls are not to be blamed here, but they should not attempt to change the rituals of the new family because the people of that house are used to them. And this is the time to show your understanding and love for the new family. There should be a mutual understanding between the two that everything else is secondary but respect for parents is primary. Respecting the parents of your partner and giving them the time and love they deserve not only strengthens your marriage but also makes it more beautiful.

This aspect is often neglected in the current times and is leading to the breakdown of many marriages. Sometimes, partners stop feeling love due to how their spouse behaves with their parents. This can lead to bitterness, which exacerbates other conflicts between them.

So, this aspect has its own role to play in deepening your love for each other. And when there is love, people are willing to change even the wrong aspects of themselves for the other person, especially when they see their partner making sincere efforts for the other family members. Believe me, it happens!

Because as they say,

"A successful marriage requires falling in love many times, always with the same person."

- Mignon McLaughlin

PARENTING

"Your kids require you most of all to love them for who they are, not to spend your whole time trying to correct them."

- Bill Ayers

In this chapter, I will primarily discuss two things: firstly, how to determine if you are ready to have kids or not, and secondly, once you have them, how to raise them to become individuals of high character.

I am writing this with the current context in mind. What I have observed happening these days is that some parents, without mutual consent and a genuine willingness to bring a child into this world, do so.

Subsequently, some parents relinquish the responsibility of wholeheartedly caring for this new relationship. In some cases, mothers leave their children in daycare for various reasons, where they may not receive the love and care they need during the crucial early stages of their development. This phenomenon is increasingly common in the modern world because both working parents find it challenging to compromise on their careers.

Bringing a new soul into this world amidst conflict will undoubtedly hurt the newborn emotionally. It is essential to sit down and discuss the decision to have a child before bringing one into the world, ensuring that both partners are on the same page and do not feel overburdened.

Your choices should not adversely affect the new life coming into this world because of you. If you fail to invest time and effort in them after the newborn arrives, you cannot expect them to flourish in life independently.

Before becoming a parent, it's crucial to understand that there is no such thing as perfect parenting. No parent can establish a universal standard for the title of "best parent." Instead of striving to be the ideal parent for your child, aim to be a natural parent.

Once the newborn arrives, allocate time to them. I emphasize this more for fathers because some new fathers assume that the sole responsibility for a child's care and love lies with the mother. Children tend to gravitate towards mothers because they receive undivided attention and love. Mothers engage with their children emotionally and create strong connections.

Although a child will always share a unique bond with the mother due to the 9-month pregnancy experience, fathers can compensate by spending more time with and becoming friends to their children.

While education is a prime focus of parents today, imparting moral values is equally important. It all begins at home.

In our Indian culture, mothers are often referred to as the 'First Teachers' of the child. Children mimic their parents' behaviour, so if the toddler exhibits good morals, acknowledging and appreciating them will encourage them to continue.

It's an important fact that children don't always follow what you say; instead, they imitate what you do. If you want them to respect others, start within your home. Demonstrating respect for your partner and others in front of them will set the right example. Creating a healthy home environment will ultimately contribute to raising a strong and well-rounded child for the future.

I have observed parents becoming irritated when their children ask many questions. However, stifling a child's curiosity early on can hinder their pursuit of science or any other field in higher studies. Therefore, never discourage your child from asking questions. Instead, guide them on the appropriate way to pose their queries.

Some parents attempt to control their children's behaviour. Instead, try to understand the belief system or emotions behind that specific behaviour and work on those aspects, which will naturally result in improved manners.

I distinctly remember how embarrassed I used to feel when my parents scolded me in front of others during my childhood. It had a lasting impact on my personality. Try not to scold your child in front of others; instead, speak politely and help them understand why they are wrong. They are more likely to respond positively.

Reflecting on my childhood, I used to play with kids whose parents granted their every request without a second thought. I often wondered why my parents couldn't do the same, and I had to persistently ask for everything I wanted.

Now, as I look back on it, I realize they were imparting a valuable life lesson: the importance of valuing money and spending it wisely. Teaching your child about finances from an early age, such as by setting a monthly allowance, is a commendable practice that parents should adopt. This will help your child learn how to save money and develop a deeper respect for it.

More than expensive gifts, your time and guidance are of greater value to your children. Although we may be living in an age dominated by smartphones, we still expect our children to learn and grow into strong individuals. However, this won't happen on its own; it requires a solid foundation established at an early age. Don't overlook this crucial aspect.

I recently came across a quote that resonated with me, and I'm sure it will resonate with you too:

"Children are not a distraction from more important work. They are the most important work."

- C.S. Lewis

MENTAL WELL BEING

"Anyone can be affected, despite their level of success or their place on the food chain. In fact, there is a good chance you know someone who is struggling with it since nearly 20% of American adults face some form of mental illness in their lifetime. So why aren't we talking about it?"

- Kristen Bell

Let's talk about the most neglected aspect of growing up: our mental well-being. At some point in our lives, we've all felt like things were spiraling out of control. There are numerous responsibilities and high expectations placed upon us, making it challenging to meet them all.

Some individuals have achieved significant milestones but still find themselves lacking the motivation to persevere. Others experience a sense of hopelessness without knowing why. We have all encountered varying degrees of mental stress and anxiety, with some even descending into the depths of depression.

We are never taught how to control our thoughts. Often, the stress we experience is a result of our minds concocting problems. However, through practice, we can cultivate the habit of recognizing that situations and their occurrence are beyond our control, whereas our actions in the present moment are within our grasp.

Our mindset plays a pivotal role in our life journey, whether we aim to achieve great heights or fear falling into the abyss of failure. The remarkable aspect is that, with practice and patience, you can cultivate a positive mindset capable of finding solutions without succumbing to panic.

Two books that profoundly influenced my mindset were 'How to Stop Worrying and Start Living' by Dale Carnegie and 'Ocean of Mind' by Manish Gaikwad. I recommend picking them up to discover how you too can transform your mindset.

I went through a period in my life when things weren't going according to plan. I was immersed in exam preparations, but progress seemed elusive. My mindset underwent changes, but thankfully, I developed habits that guided me through this challenging phase.

The most helpful habit I cultivated was self-reflection. You can do this too through meditation, which increases your awareness of your thoughts.

Meditation is just one avenue; you can also spend time in nature, connecting with the universe's soul, and introspect. When nothing seems to go your way, consider aligning with a higher power. If you feel your inner turmoil escalating, surround yourself with people who can recharge your positive energy.

If you lack such individuals in your life, your best option is to choose five books that can reshape your beliefs. When you're stressed or overwhelmed, what you need most is an alternative perspective to navigate through the challenges.

I've witnessed people taking drastic measures in their lives, often failing to recognize the value of this beautiful gift of life. I have a saying for everyone: "Never stop seeking solutions to your problems." Some moments should not define your entire life; do not take them too seriously. Approach each phase as just that—a phase in your life, not your entire existence. Similarly, a challenging situation or a low point is just that—a moment in life, not the entirety of it. Your future depends on how you handle and perceive these situations, so maintain a positive outlook in every life circumstance. Remind yourself:

"This too shall Pass."

(Ye waqt bhi guzar jayega.)

Something great awaits me on my life's journey.

If you think you are stressed today because you have less money in your account, believe me, the ones who have more aren't dancing on the roads. It's the poor kid who dances on the roads and enjoys the first rain of monsoon.

Not being able to crack an exam, not being able to get the dream job, not being able to build a career, someone left me, I left someone, had a fight with someone, or anything that is giving you stress—just sit and take a break to think: Is that your entire life?

Taking a pause will give your mind space to think for you instead of dwelling on all the negative thoughts that may never materialize.

"*We are nothing more than the repeated thoughts created in our minds.*"

If you feel stressed because you don't have a particular thing in life, think of those who wish to have a life like yours. Okay, let me tell you one interesting story.

Once, a man was sitting in front of a 5-star hotel. He was eating a sandwich while watching people go inside the hotel.

He started thinking about them and how lucky they were to enjoy a life like this. Thinking, thinking, and thinking, he suddenly became so sad that he started to lament his poor life. He threw away his sandwich, then headed toward his vehicle. Suddenly, he turned and saw an old man and his daughter running to pick up the sandwich he had thrown. This moved him deeply. He then thought about how God had given him so much, and instead of being grateful for it, he regretted what he did not have. From that day onwards, he never cried for what he did not have; rather, he treasured what he had.

If you face such a situation, spend time with your loved ones, giggle with them, get involved in activities that will keep you active. This won't take away all your concerns at once, but taking a step for yourself will inspire you, for life is not that hard to live cheerfully.

If you ever feel stressed or down, never isolate yourself because the more we separate ourselves from others, the more the mind plays tricks on us and makes us feel lonely and powerless.

I want to conclude all my words above with this thought to contemplate:

"Our outer version is the reflection of our inner thoughts."

FINANCIAL FREEDOM

"It's not how much money you make, but how much money you keep, how hard it works for you, and how many generations you keep it for."

- Robert Kiyosaki

The harrowing fact of the education system, of which we are the products and future generations will also emerge from, is its purpose to mold us into employees capable of mass production. We are essentially paying to become just that, and while it's a tough reality to digest, we are all living it.

I have never studied a single subject during my school days that taught me how to deal with real-life problems. All you and I had to do was cram up some stuff to pass the exams. But what about the problems that we face in the dynamic world? They don't care if you are a topper or a failure. All they see is what value you are adding to the lives of other people right now.

Today, with such a vast workforce and competition, you will forever remain a newcomer unless you acquire real-world skills. Consider a young graduate who has just left college and wishes to start their own business. However, because they were taught nothing about it in their entire education, they don't know how to begin or raise funds.

Most of us come from lower or upper-middle-class backgrounds and bear the brunt of this situation more. But this should never be your excuse for not growing. So, if you are serious about achieving financial freedom in your life, then follow some principles consistently. Take notes because I will discuss money next.

If you want to grow your wealth, do not rely on a single income source. Invest in your skills and start a business alongside it or create multiple income sources for yourself.

Change your circle of association if it is hindering your path to financial freedom. Begin spending time with people who have achieved financial freedom in their lives and who motivate you to do the same.

If you say that you have no such people, then pick up any five books on financial freedom. Read. Read and Read. Then start applying what you have read in your life because that matters the most.

To start, consider reading 'The Intelligent Investor,' 'Rich Dad, Poor Dad,' 'Think and Grow Rich,' 'The Psychology of Money,' and 'The Richest Man in Babylon.'

'The Richest Man in Babylon' will even teach you about the marvels that compound interest can bring into your life, as it is often referred to as the "8th wonder of the world." I could go on about it, but that would digress us. I will surely try to write a book on it in the future with your love and support.

When I mention financial freedom, don't assume that I am only talking about a job that provides you with a fixed salary at the end of every month. Financial freedom means that your money should be able to generate wealth even when you are sleeping. However, it does not mean that you will not have to work anymore.

This will require a significant shift in your mindset about money. The first change needs to be in how you repel money with negative thoughts about it, for instance, thinking it is hard to earn. Once you start doing that, you will move closer to attaining financial freedom by loving money more and earning more of it.

You will begin to enjoy your financial freedom and even become a source of income for many others around you.

People often assume that when someone talks about financial freedom, they are referring to saving money. But saving money alone cannot bring financial freedom. What you need is to INVEST. Now, many of you might assume that I am talking about investing money in the stock market.

No, that is not the only way to invest your money. If you don't want to put your money in a risky place, consider investing in real estate, starting a business, pursuing an idea, or providing solutions to social problems. Invest in upgrading your skills. You never think twice about spending on your pleasures and treasures in life, but you will overthink a thousand times before buying that one book that can change your thinking forever.

When we talk about investing money, we mean placing your money where it can generate income for you after you have invested it. Investing in creating assets will generate more income sources that can cover your additional expenses.

Some people take out loans and then invest them. I consider two types of loans to exist. If you take out a loan to build assets, then they are good loans. However, if you use the loan amount to buy liabilities, they are bad loans that add nothing to your assets.

For example, if you borrow 20 lakhs from a bank to buy a car and spend it all at once, that's not a productive use of the loan. Alternatively, you could invest that money in buying a house, rent it out, and create an additional income source for yourself. The rent you receive can then be saved to buy a car, and you also have a house that covers your extra expenses.

That's the magic of financial freedom. I believe that money is all about circulation.

Here's another quote by Suze Orman for you to reflect upon:

"A big part of financial freedom is having our heart and mind free from worry about the 'What Ifs' of life."

TIME MANAGEMENT

"Being rich is having money, being wealthy is having time."

– Margret Boonnano

Everyone around you often claims to be as busy as a bee and hardly having any time. I have realized that only 5 to 10 per cent of people are genuinely utilizing their time productively. People around me frequently complain that they have no spare time for even their families. However, on the other hand, they are frequently wasting it.

To no one's surprise, they are constantly scrolling through their phones, being active on social media while telling others how busy they are. This life is yours, and choosing how to live it also lies in your hands. You can either spend it recklessly and leave it behind one day, or you can make a mark in the world so that you are remembered even after your departure.

You must have heard these lines, *"It does not matter whether you lived a long life; what matters is whether you lived a big life."* The quality of your life matters more than the number of years you spend on this earth. Time is the factor that can make or break the quality of your life. If you have added value to the life of even one person on this earth, you can surely have the feeling of a '*life well spent.*' But if you are just pretending to be busy, then you need a shift in your mindset and should focus more on time management.

At the end of the day, you should not go to sleep in regret over a wasted day. Rather than discussing how some of us fail in managing time, let's talk about a new concept that can help you a long way. **Time Freedom** is one such concept that is widely used to live a life that allows you to work even if you are not physically present at your workplace.

If you work in a company, you usually have to be physically present there to earn that day's salary for the work you do. However, if you understand the concept of time freedom and start applying it in your life and career, you will be able to work without being physically present.

For instance, Jeff Bezos, the owner of Amazon, can change his location, but that won't stop Amazon from running. In the same way, apply time freedom so your work can continue, even in your absence. Creating a system that helps you become time-independent enables you to manage your time wisely. It will run your work on autopilot so you can focus on growth and exploring new aspects of life.

If you look at successful businessmen like Ratan Tata Ji or Mukesh Ambani Ji, how much time do you think they have? They have as much time as the number of employees they have working for them. Once you start experiencing this freedom of time, you will also become a source of income for other people, all while enjoying the freedom it brings to your own life. It will create a brand that will continue even after you are gone.

I emphasize this because I believe, "*The goal should not be to make more money; the goal should be to live life on your terms.*"

And this can be achieved, even when you are working a job. Work on building a side career for yourself. Use your time wisely and create a system that works for you, allowing you to have time not just for your growth but for your family and loved ones as well. Achieving a balance between Self, Family, Work, and Social life is the goal.

To reach this stage of time freedom, managing your current time is where you need to start working now. I would suggest that if you want to delve deeper into time management, read these books: "Time Management," "The 7 Habits of Highly Effective People," and "Eat That Frog." Because unless you manage your time, you can't manage your life.

Start by applying the 8-8-8 rule where you allocate 8 hours for sleep, 8 hours for work, and 8 hours for leisure. Alternatively, if that feels too challenging, apply the 6+6+6+6 rule: sleep for 6 hours, work for 6 hours, spend 3 hours with your family, allocate 2 hours for personal time, and dedicate 1 hour to self-development, which sums up to another 6 hours. The remaining 6 hours can be divided for 2 hours of social media, 2 hours of entertainment, and 2 hours for meditation, exercises, yoga, or walks. This is a flexible schedule that can be adjusted to suit your needs.

You can even break down your work priorities, but what's more important is to plan and execute them the next day. This will help you keep track of where you spend the most time and identify if it's being wasted. If it is, take wise steps to rectify it. This will further help you eliminate distractions and prioritize your work.

You can also set daily targets and create a to-do list if following a schedule doesn't work for you. If putting *tick marks* on the to-do list motivates you, then go for it. But keep auditing yourself and reviewing the results, so you can have clarity on your goals and the action plan you need. Throughout this process, remember to respect other people's time as you do your own, so they can reciprocate the same.

I have something to conclude with, a thought for you to ponder:

"Real wealth is all about freedom, whether its money, time or location...Freedom to choose to live your life as you love to live."

Part 3
Mid-Life Crisis

GENERATION GAP

"The gap between generations arises because a young person looks at the future, a middle-aged person looks at the present and an old person looks at the past."

- M.S.Rao

Nothing is permanent, but change is the only constant. Everybody knows this, but still, what often happens is that our grandparents do not understand our parents, our parents don't understand us, and maybe we won't understand our children and vice-versa. What follows is often conflict.

Conflict is not inherently bad; it is normal to have conflicts. However, the problem arises when ego gets in the way. There are some misconceptions in younger generations that they can change the older ones.

Think wisely, is that possible? And can it be done in a day? Suppose you are 20 years old, and your parents are 50 years old. You want to change a fifty-year-old mindset when you can't even change your own twenty-year-old thinking. And don't worry, I am not going to talk about changing your thinking.

But I am surely going to talk about understanding and taking small steps to support each other because it is easy to advise but difficult to support. Only those who love can provide true support.

I am not going to offer advice only to the older generation, but I have been observing something common in youngsters nowadays. They lose patience over small things, like someone asking them a question more than once, especially if that person is their parent. They often forget that they annoyed their parents as children by asking repeated questions because they understood the world less. If parents had shown the same irritation, they would not have gained initial knowledge.

Taking your parents for granted, or parents do not understand their child's point of view, creates a wider gap between the two. But instead of focusing on the problem, let us explore what can be done in such situations.

If you always keep in mind that your relationship with your loved ones is more important, I don't think the generation gap can create conflicts that can't be resolved. Even if there are conflicts, respecting each other should not be compromised. Always consider supporting each other even after stating your opinions.

Patience is key when dealing with people. If you see that things are turning sour, it is always better to take a pause at that time or stay quiet and continue the discussion later. Holding your views is never wrong in any relationship, regardless of your age, but respecting the other person's perspective is equally important. In short, if you take a step forward, the other person may take two.

I have a lot to say to parents too about how parenting is not just another responsibility but a wise decision that is demanding. You can read my thoughts on it in the chapter on Parenting.

Sometimes, parents are overprotective of their children. This is often because many don't understand the difference between attachment and love. If you are too attached to something, and in this case, we are talking about children, you may try to impose your thoughts to keep them safe. But if you truly love them, as you do, then you should let your child bloom.

Because saying it is a generation gap and your children have gone astray is not the solution. As the bigger person, you have to demonstrate it too. We know that your generation often had to save 20 rupees by walking for 20 minutes, while your child may spend 20 rupees to save 20 minutes. That's how things have changed. Acknowledge this change, and instead of creating a fuss about it, accept that lifestyles evolve with time.

The younger generation has much to learn too. Their parents came from a time of big joint families and had little privacy. For them, those were the best days, and we have to admit that today's generation is more focused on accumulating money than on collective living. So, you cannot entirely dismiss their opinions when it comes to considering everyone's perspective before making life decisions. They are wired that way because they lived that way for years.

All you can do is create an environment of conversation at home because that is the only safe space you and your parents have. Today, even children have to realize that parents can never think ill of their children, and it is the only selfless relationship you have in this world.

Learning from each other's experiences is all you should aim for in this life, where you are born to live and love. Build a bridge to bridge the generation gap. A bridge of communication, collaboration, and support for each other's happiness. And I strongly believe,

"There will be no generation gap if there is a bridge of communication, collaboration, and support to back each other."

WRINKLES OF LIFE

"If wrinkles must be written on our brows, let them not be written upon the heart. The spirit should never grow old."

- James A. Garfield

As you age, you go through many bodily changes, and it shows on your face as well. This can be quite stressful for many people because it is hard to accept that you are growing older. It is difficult to leave behind the youth and enthusiasm you once had. Sometimes you become much more nostalgic by thinking about your younger days. But shouldn't this be a phase you can be proud of? Looking back, you can see how far you have come and how much you have evolved as a person.

If we talk about the biological changes that aging people go through, there is a wide range of hormonal shifts, changes in bone density, digestive system issues, visual and hearing difficulties, and wrinkly skin. Though not a problem, it makes many of us conscious about our changing looks. It is hard to see our beauty diminishing with each passing year. But this is a very natural thing that happens to everyone.

Even our ancestors in India were conscious about aging, and that's why we had products like *Chyavanprash* made by Rishi Chyavana.

Aging is natural but can be slowed down if we make certain changes in our lifestyle. As you age, you should include some exercise routines like aerobics, yoga, walking, jogging, or meditation. Your diet and sleep time also play an equal role in a healthy aging process.

The hard part is when you have lived with your habits for such a long time. However, I don't believe that you cannot make some changes for your health. All those habits that are harmful should be minimized at the right time so you don't have to give them up all at once when the doctor advises you to, which is the hardest part.

Our ancestors were right in talking about moving towards renunciation, which means leaving things slowly and steadily. It should be practiced as you realize that you have started aging. The more you practice it, the easier it becomes to let go of things for the betterment of your health.

We are often very careful about the health of every family member, but when it comes to ourselves, we become lazy. If not all, then some surely do so. Especially mothers who are aging often neglect or do not prioritize themselves. Here's a suggestion: you should at least get a health checkup once a year if you can't go for regular ones.

When we age, we also experience a lot of stress, which seems inevitable. Be it our children, their careers, their marriages, and whatnot. This stress affects our mental, emotional, and physical health. Studies have shown how psychological stress affects our limbic and prefrontal cortex, which is the area in humans that regulates emotional well-being.

So, it becomes very important in this age and time to realize that taking stress is not the solution; instead, it can lead to more mental and emotional problems. You should understand that even though your children are growing, they need you more than ever, even if they may not say so.

I have seen many people in my life who have crossed the age of 60 and still look young and fresh. Then you realize that it is not their bodies that appear young, but their attitude and how they are enjoying this phase of life. You too can spread the same freshness all around, but only when you eat right and think right.

I would recommend reading the book 'Wabi Sabi' by Beth Kempton. It will surely teach you how to stay happy and enjoy every phase of life. Even in 'Ikigai' by Francesc Miralles and Hector Garcia, many people who have lived longer than the average human have explained their secrets to a longer life.

Many people realized their unfulfilled dreams from their younger years. Some are traveling now, some are painting, and some are learning the skills that they couldn't learn when they had so many responsibilities on their shoulders. Don't worry about the days gone by, but look forward to the days that are yet to come. Because you know what, "The best wrinkle is a SMILE."

BABY PLANNING

Parenting is a lifetime job and does not stop when a child grows up."

–Jake Slope

You must be wondering why we named this chapter "Baby Planning." Because of obvious reasons. The babies you brought into this world will always remain your babies.

You do not even realize when and how those little ones turn into teenagers and complete their schooling and college life. So, technically speaking, they are no longer babies. But you can't stop thinking of them that way as parents.

From the teachings of Shri Krishna in the Bhagavad Gita, I have realized that you should not focus on building a comfortable life for your children. Instead, think of making them good in character and full of life.

You cannot predict the good or bad times in your kids' future, but if you educate them with the right Samskaras and build them as strong individuals of good character, they will know how to handle those situations and how to remain strong in times of need.

Parents usually think that it is their prerogative to choose their child's career path, life partner, or future job or business. They often forget that attachment and love have different meanings and outcomes.

Any decision you make for them, if it cannot secure a good future where they are happy and satisfied, can never be taken out of love but only out of pure attachment.

Always remember that *"Love gives you rights and liberates you, but attachment takes away rights and enslaves you."*

Usually, parents at this stage worry about their children's careers, whether they will be well-settled, have a good job, and be happily married.

But believe me, instead of worrying about their life and future, if you focus on educating them about the difference between right and wrong, help them understand truth from lies, and teach them the correct way to think about others and for others, they will develop an understanding of how to handle their lives and its challenges.

You may not need to worry much about their intelligence. I have seen many parents who have mentally and emotionally crippled their children by providing them with all the comforts of life and dictating every decision in their lives, which ultimately turns their children into rebels when they grow up.

Again, I am going to talk about lessons from the Bhagavad Gita, which teaches us that if we want to think about our children, we should focus on how they develop patience, love, and remain positive in every life situation.

More importantly, teach them to think in the right way by removing negative thoughts and thinking positively, because everything depends on thoughts.

Your thoughts can become your well-wishers, but if they turn negative, they become your biggest enemies. Communicating this to your children in the right manner becomes crucial in this ongoing stressful era.

As I discussed in the previous chapter on the generation gap, the more you create an environment of conversation in your home, the less impact the generation gap will be. This is the best inheritance you can give your children.

And as Shiv Khera says, "*Good parenting gives headaches, but bad parenting gives heartaches.*" So always try to focus on giving Samskaras that you can be proud of. And if you are unable to see them in your children, it is time to stop and look at their associations, surroundings, and activities. But don't forget to also look in the mirror because sometimes your children can become your reflection unknowingly.

JEEVANSATHI

"The best thing to hold onto in life is each other."

– Audrey

I have seen many partners grow with age, fighting with each other over petty things. This becomes like their daily ritual, and they cannot begin their day without a fight. Sometimes, these small fights take ugly turns, leading couples to get divorced even after spending years together.

This phenomenon seems to be happening more nowadays, perhaps because responsibilities increase, and couples do not spend as much time together as they did when they were young and passionate about each other. Some people who entered relationships at a young age out of physical attraction often grow apart as the initial spark fades. Additionally, with aging, they go through many bodily and behavioural changes.

However, some researchers have stated that as people age, their need for a partner increases. A healthy relationship brings happiness, which enhances the chances of success in life compared to when there is constant conflict within a family or with a spouse.

I have discussed in earlier chapters about love and relationships and how you can make your bond stronger even after going through changes. The stronger the bond between you and your partner, the easier it is to resolve conflicts that arise due to differences.

No one can ever say that they never have conflicts, no matter how strong their bond is. What's important here is to resolve your differences and not let them linger due to ego. Ego should never be a permanent barrier between people who have decided to spend their lives together.

As you age, it becomes more important to maintain a happy marriage because it affects your children. The love between you two will define love for your children, and they will judge the world based on those parameters.

I've observed that as people enter this age bracket, they start becoming conscious that their partner may no longer be interested in them and doesn't find them attractive anymore. This can lead to anxiety and irritation between the couple. However, the solution is simple: communicate openly with your partner about your feelings.

Why do you need your partner more than ever now? As you transition from youth to middle age, your children are moving towards independence, getting married, and building their families. This can create an emptiness in life that your partner can relate to. You both become emotionally and physically dependent on each other.

So, resolve those conflicts because you've already spent a significant portion of your lives together and created many memories, along with your children. It's beautiful to sit and recollect those memories as they bring you closer and create a sense of gratitude for the life you've shared.

You should sit together and recall the challenging times when you were there for each other and faced life's challenges as a team.

I recommend reading these two books on relationships that I enjoyed: "The Secret of Relationships" by Rhonda Byrne and "Loving Your Spouse When You Feel Like Walking Away" by Gary Chapman. They will surely enhance your views about your partner.

If you can calmly and happily reach this stage of life, you can work out minor difficulties between each other. Sometimes, I feel that romance is overrated, and what truly stays with you at the end is loyalty and the friendship you've built over time.

With unconditional time for each other, you can create more happiness and provide eternal support. I've seen people who have lost their partners in accidents and living each day without them feels like a life without purpose for many. If you can see your partner's face every morning, be grateful. Life becomes more beautiful when you've lived it for others, not just for yourself.

Always remember, "*Love doesn't need to be perfect; it just has to be true.*"

Coconut to Cream

"The maturity is not measured by the number of years you lived, but by the depth of wisdom gained, the compassion cultivated, and the ability to navigate life's challenges with Grace."

Close your eyes and recall your youth. Let's not focus on the bright memories for a while; instead, imagine the changes you have gone through. Can you see yourself getting angry over small problems? I'm sure you're imagining the times when you were the most hyper version of yourself, when you picked fights over petty issues, and when you engaged in the ugliest arguments of your life just out of ego.

Now open your eyes and look at yourself in the mirror. You are no longer the same person. You don't lose your temper; instead, you face every challenge in a calm and composed manner. You no longer indulge in arguments; rather, you prefer to stay quiet and prioritize peace over long and tiring explanations because you now understand that it's useless to educate unless someone is genuinely interested.

You can see how much you have changed as a person. You have matured with age, although age is not the only reason for maturity. Your age and life experiences have made you an understanding being. Now, every decision you make considers others, but there was a time when you couldn't recognize the difference between those who were your own and those who were backstabbers. Now, you have a close group that you have realized are your well-wishers.

Perhaps with time, you have started believing in the universe or a higher power. Some even become more spiritual as they realize that throughout their lives, they planned and planned, but life happened while they were busy planning. Someone up there is controlling everything, and that's why you can't plan life. You are just a medium. Thoughts about your existence and purpose start taking up space in your brain. You become more compassionate with time, start caring for others, donate to the needy often, feed the hungry, and do small things that bring you joy.

Every man or woman, in the early days of their life, is hard and rough like the shell of a coconut. But with age and maturity, they start shedding that shell and move towards the creamy part of their life where they begin experiencing the softer version of themselves. That's why I named this chapter "From Coconut to Cream." Your journey from an unpolished rock to a polished idol begins, and your achievements, hard work, and success become an inspiration for the younger ones around you. Then comes the age of sharing your experiences with those younger than you.

At this age, you should focus on giving back to the society that gave you so much when you were young and inexperienced. Be ready to work a little differently because you become more of a living philosopher for the people around you, holding wise experiences in life. This age is the time when you should share them with everyone you encounter so you can give them food for thought.

Because someone once said, "*Aging is just another word for living.*"

FEAR: NOTHING TO LOSE

"We came into this world with nothing, and we leave with nothing, don't boast if you have everything because it's just temporary."

Life is going smoothly, and suddenly some thoughts hits you hard. That hard hit is the thought that you have turned 40, 50, 60, or so on. Then you start thinking about what has been achieved so far and what hasn't. Many ideas surround you, one after another.

You may regret that you had a plan almost ready, and you couldn't accomplish it. Or you have spent an entire life with someone you never wanted to marry in the first place. You might even think that half of your life is already spent, and all you did was think about your children and your family.

When this realization hits, you think about how you have finished a major chunk of your life thinking and overthinking for another person's happiness, but it was not reciprocated to you with the same passion. You never considered your desires, your enjoyment, and your preferences. All these thoughts create a fear that activates the thinking that you cannot start anything new and big now. You then start questioning yourself if this is all that you wanted in your life. You may even start questioning your presence and the purpose in this life.

Our soul is ageless. It stays young even as our bodies age. The soul wants to explore and experience life, to create memories, but our bodies have started withering with age. When we are not able to do what our soul truly wants us to make, it leads to fears of losing strength, beauty, or anything precious to our material desires, thus leading to overthinking.

We see everything transforming around us quickly. Our lovely children leaving us and settling into their lives. Our close ones changing priorities, and then we have fears of loneliness coming around now and then, accompanying the fears of losing respect sometimes.

There can be varying reasons for these fears that may arise during the middle of your life. But let us discuss some thought cycles so that you do not take this as a crisis but as a new step in your life.

If you have latent dreams, then all you need to understand is that these fears are all a sham. First things first, you must know yourself from within. Know the risks that you can take now. Some can take risks in life at 30 while some at 50. You need to remind yourself that in the past, you began with zero and achieved so much in life. You can do it once more.

Think as if all you have is this life, and living it to the fullest is what matters for your soul and you too. Don't find your happiness in others; instead, create your own bliss by removing all these fears. If your children are discovering their own enjoyment and creating their own little world, instead of chasing after them for time, love, and respect, do what you love to do. Learn to spend time with yourself. Make a list of places you wanted to visit but couldn't because of responsibilities.

Remember that your body is what makes you live in this world. Regular exercise, Yoga, walks, and meditation can keep you energized for life ahead. If you have always wanted to read all the world's books but time was a limitation, pick a book now. I would recommend that you read '*Quarter Life Crisis.*'

If you have a feeling that a lot is yet to be accomplished, then I believe your time has come. Some make it big in their 40s, some in their 50s, and some in their 60s. *Grandma Moses* was not painted until she was 77 years old and became a famous American artist after age of 77, a dream she was predestined to fulfill.

Always remember,

"Nothing is permanent in this world except birth and death."

AGE IS JUST A NUMBER

"Anyone who stops learning is old, whether at 20 or 80. Anyone who keeps learning stays young. The greatest thing in life is to keep your mind young." -Henry Ford

The quote above reminds me that it's never too late to do what makes your heart sing. People who have had great adventures in life weren't restricted by age. *Christopher Columbus* was 41 when he discovered America. His life was not confined to the digits on the calendar but fueled by the fire within his soul.

If you want to experiment at this phase of life, as *Nike* says, *just do it.* Chase unfulfilled dreams now because you have the time to invest completely new energy with a vast understanding of life. Don't bother about what others will say. They have always said something, right?

If *Colonel Sanders* had thought that he was too old, he wouldn't have founded KFC at 62. Or if Mark Zuckerberg had thought he was too young at 19, there would be no Facebook.

Just go ahead, chase your dreams, and embrace the new adventures of your life. You have all the wisdom of life; all you need is to seize the opportunity. It is time to establish that age is just a number.

So far, you ran a rat race; now it's time to run a different one and set yourself free from society's expectations. But make some preparations ahead. Start by creating balance in your routine and building a diet chart so that you can feel young and fit for a new inning of life.

Your entire life and your experiences have lessons that can inspire many. I have realized while reading *Ikigai* that life is an endless process rather than a stationary destination.

If your age stops you from learning new skills, starting a new business, or launching that YouTube channel you have yearned for, just remember that the scariest thought would be to make the same mistake of not beginning what your heart desires over and over.

Make plans, associate with like-minded people who inspire you, and execute your thoughts. Like I have said earlier in the previous chapter, your soul is ageless. This quality it holds helps you, but only if you stop counting and start living every moment prosperously while chasing the purpose that you desire forever.

As Mark Twain said,

"Age is an issue of mind over matter. If you don't mind it doesn't matter."

CHAAR LOG

"Caring About What Others Think of You Is A Waste of Time. Most People Don't Have A Clue What to Think of Themselves."

- Zane Baker

The biggest disease we all have is, "Why aren't people pleased with us?" This human mind can never stop thinking. But the biggest headache comes when you think more about what others will say about you rather than what you think about yourself. Some people are never able to live their lives freely because of these thoughts. Some are not able to point out the wrongs freely, and some are trapped in a rat race forever.

Remember that the fear of judgment can limit you from reaching your highest potential and can rob you of the joy that comes with being true to yourself. I have seen many who, because of this fear alone, were not able to work on their dreams, their lives, or anything they wished for. Even though they were not hurting anyone, they were stuck with these thoughts.

If you know that your decision will lead to your inner happiness and it is for the greater good, take that decision because regrets are the worst. You can keep people around you happy only when you are content inside.

Believe me, in the end, what will matter the most is who you are, where you are, and with whom you are. You will search for satisfaction, which comes only when you do not care about others but for yourself first. I am not asking you to think only about yourself and not care about others at all. But prioritizing yourself keeps you busy and happy in the end.

Because I feel that even if you have all the world's riches, the perfect life partner, all the smartness and beauty, and if you are not happy inside, if you are not peaceful inside, nothing matters.

We often don't take that first step thinking about what four people (char log) say, but I want to ask you, who are those four people? And when you or anyone in your family needs some help, where are these people who are always the focus of your decision-making when you do something for yourself?

I believe that the only people who deserve to stay with you in your happy times are the ones who were there for you in your worst times. People who were laughing at you when you were a failure, or people who moved away because you were nothing, should have no significance in the first place.

If you are putting your energy into listening to them, then you will never reach your destination. Assume your life as a car. You are the driver, and you have four more people sitting with you inside. One asks to take the left, the other to the right. The third says to go straight ahead, and the fourth one wants to go back. Will you ever reach your destination?

Instead of putting all your focus and energy on people who provide zero value to your life, focus your energy on going deeper and knowing your purpose while working on it. Take this decision now because it is never too late. Be your own biggest critic and your biggest supporter as well.

Let people think what they want to; it's their job. You do yours and work on yourself.

And if this still bothers you, then read these lines I found online (credits to the writer).

"I used to care what people thought about me until I tried to pay my bills with their opinions."

No More Regrets

"I look back and I have no regrets, truly, everything led me to the place where I am now."

– Wendy Whelan

The most frightening thing in life is to regret the past. Little do we realize that living a life without regrets is not about erasing your past or avoiding mistakes in the future.

Having no regrets means embracing your journey with all its ups and downs, healing throughout the process, and forgiving everyone, including yourself. By letting go of your guilt, you make space to live freely and can fully direct your thoughts toward the purpose, joy, happiness, peace, and bliss you deserve.

Only when you let go of your fears or guilt from the past can you experience the possibilities and create room for new things to happen in your life. Usually, people recall the past and create scenarios in their minds of the alternatives they should have pursued or think of the wrong decisions they could have avoided, but that is simply a waste of the present moment too.

It stops you from acting in the moment and reduces your chance of success in the future as well. Have you ever wondered why we regret so much? It is always wisest to know the reason behind the problem before discussing the solution.

We have regrets because we keep expectations, be it from family, people, or society. When we set aside our happiness and do things as per others' wishes and do not get reciprocated equally, we go into a spiral of regrets for choosing others' happiness over ours.

As humans, we make mistakes, but regrets occur only when, instead of learning from our mistakes, we focus more on the mistake itself. It is said that when you are full of regrets, LET GO and LET GOD. The only way to come out of this bag of regrets is to focus on yourself, your goals, and your vision while not thinking ill of anyone. When you are unable to control things in your life and your past has made it all worse, and it seems that someone else is controlling your life completely differently, trust the universe.

I would say that when this happens, sit and meditate on your goals and place all your concentration on achieving them without thinking about the results for a while. Whatever the result is, accept it as God's wish.

Also, you will have to stop focusing on one moment or one incident of your life and stop considering it as your entire life. Stop whining about what you do not have and instead be happy and appreciative of what you have. I would suggest that you read the book 'The Top Five Regrets of

Dying' by Bronnie Ware. This book will help you cherish your present more than ever.

When people cry about the past or worry about the future, I tell them this very beautiful story.

Once, a lion asks a squirrel to cut a sack. If she cuts a smaller sack, she gets some peanuts, but if she cuts the most enormous sack, she gets a bag full of peanuts.

The squirrel, instead of focusing on what she can get now, thinks about a bag full of peanuts that she can have in the future. She starts trimming the most giant sack. When she is done, the lion gives her the hefty bag of peanuts. The joy that she feels, she has never felt it before. She has never gained this big in her life.

She is about to open the bag of peanuts when a realization dawns upon her that all her teeth are worn out from cutting the bigger sack, and she cannot eat the peanuts now.

This is what most of us do. We focus more on the past or future and stop living in the moment. We are so focused on a well-established future or a bank balance that when the time comes for us to freely enjoy the wealth we have earned, we no longer have the will or wish left to do it.

But I will say it again, if you have done all that I spoke about above, you should still have no regrets. You have this instant to enjoy and make shifts in your life.

I want to repeat what Milla Vane once said:

"Make the best use of what you have. Waste no time with wishes and regrets."

HAPPILY, EVER AFTER

"There is no path to happiness, happiness is the path."

– Buddha

You must have noticed some funny titles in the previous chapters. Want to know why I did that? So that a smile spreads across your face while reading them.

In the end, what matters is whether you are happy or not. If you are happy with yourself and the people around you, believe me, no one is luckier than you in this world.

Happiness is not there all the time, or it is not ready to come whenever you want it; instead, happiness is a choice you have to make. You do it through your thoughts and actions.

If you start cherishing every small moment of your life and keep that smile intact, you will see that the world around you is not the same as before.

Have you ever wondered why people experience grief? Because situations don't turn out as they want them to, and people become unhappy, be it in relationships, a job, business, or any exam. Do you know if you learn to accept the situation as it is, nothing can make you feel wretched? Of course, I am not talking about accepting any harassment or cruelty because that is an extreme situation, but the situations where you can find solutions by keeping cool.

At some point, I feel that it is for the best that not everything happens as we wish because if that had been the case, this world would have been a messy place.

You can always start being happy within yourself; then, only people around you can feel the happiness. Because if you are empty inside and full of worries, what will you offer to the world around you? You will always give what you have. So, create happiness within, and you will have only happiness to give around.

We always place conditions on our happiness by attaching them to situations. For instance, if I get this person in life, I will be happy. If I get this job, then only I will be happy, or the day I buy this car, I will be happy, and so on.

You must have seen people saying to you sometimes, "Why are you happy without any reason?" Well, that is how it should be. You should be happy without any reason.

Once you start conditioning your happiness, it becomes a way of life, and soon every smile will be a smile for a reason. This is not the right way to live a blissful life.

Life is a journey from womb to tomb. And this journey is experienced differently by each one of us. Some can be very excited about this, some a little less.

Take this life as a snake and ladder game. The way you play it with your family, with some fights, some laughter. The same has to be done with life too.

After the game is over, what do you enjoy the most? The fun you had during the play. Right? And if you do not have that fun, you will never play the game again. The same holds true for life; having fun makes it bearable.

No one can promise you a hundred per cent sorrow-proof life. Not even God. But who can make it memorable for us? We. We make a life that gives us satisfaction at the end. And the more you enjoy this journey, the more your satisfaction will be on your deathbed.

I am putting my pen down with this chapter, but I have something crucial to say in the end. Our present actions make our future, but always remember that we are a part of the higher consciousness, which is not only our Father but also our Mother too. If, even after all your efforts, you cannot achieve what you wanted to, then the higher consciousness has a better plan for you than yours.

Because, as they say, God can see what our eyes cannot.

Always remember,

"Happiness is not about getting all you want, it is about enjoying all you have."

AUTHOR'S NOTE

Our Life Is A Magic

"The day I decided that my life was magical, there was suddenly magic all around me."

A thought. It is a single word, but this single word, '*a thought,*' can change your entire life. Everything starts with a thought. Whatever miraculous or impossible things you see people doing around you started with a thought, an idea.

I have always believed that you can achieve anything you want with the power of your thoughts. If you read biographies of people who succeeded in achieving their dreams, you will realize that the only difference there was their thought process.

Your thoughts decide your reactions to situations and your action plan for your life. The clearer your thoughts, the closer you get to your purpose in life. As the saying goes, "*What you think, you become. What you feel, you attract. What you imagine, you create.*"

Mostly people remain in the rat race because they never attain clarity in their thoughts. People often talk about another person's success. They talk about how lucky some people are to have what they dreamt of.

But no one focuses on their zero-to-hero journey. I am sure you are not one of those people since you chose to read this book. Stop focusing on excuses like luck because luck is not isolated. Come out of your comfort zone and don't sit and make opinions; instead, strive to be the talk of the show.

If I talk about myself, I know that it was my thoughts that changed my life completely. A few years back, I read a book called 'The Secret.' This book taught me that I can achieve anything. Then began the journey of reading more and more. The books I read made me realize that my thoughts can help me stand apart from the crowd.

Living and dying are not in our hands, but the time between the two is totally within our control. To make the best out of it is up to us. So, when someone writes about you in the future, they should write with full pride.

People who did unique things in life had their share of troubles and struggles too. Nothing came easy to them. The bigger the dream, the bigger the hurdles. Even the universe tests them to know if they truly deserve what they dream of. So, if you dream big, get ready for the bigger test on your way.

But the day the universe believes that you deserve it, it will start helping you achieve your mission. It will start removing from your life, all your hurdles and those people who are not right for your journey, even if you want them in your life. The universe will not let anything wrong happen to you. It may remove some people and some happy moments, but it will give back something better that you could not have gotten for yourself ever. Just trust its intelligence.

All you need to do is work on your thoughts, make them positive, believe in yourself, have gratitude for all the goodness in life, and keep working for your purpose. Accept every decision as the decision of the higher consciousness and keep moving.

Our life is magic, and our thoughts are the magical magnets. All we need is to choose wisely the right thoughts that can bring about the appropriate changes in our lives. I would like all of you to read the book 'The Magic.'

I always suggest books because I think books are the biggest treasure one can have in life. Learning from other people's experiences and finding solutions to your life situations are a boon to mankind.

I want to end this note by saying that people often think what matters the most is whether you are successful or not. But what matters more is how many people are successful in their lives because of you or how many people succeeded with your support.

Because once you start living for others, no one can stop you from being the happiest in your life and achieving whatever you want. Keep collecting blessings because they will take you higher and higher. These blessings will bring satisfaction to your life, and your face will reflect it. Your life will reflect it, and you will reflect it when you leave this world with a smile of gratification.

"Our life is magic and our thoughts are magical magnets, so pay attention to your thoughts and choose them wisely & take action accordingly."

ABOUT THE AUTHOR

Neelam singh is an Indian businesswoman, investor, philanthropist and writer.

Neelam Singh hails from a city called Faridabad in Haryana, India. She has garnered much acclaim for her Startup Centillionaires Ardor Industry Pvt Ltd. also known as ceNdor Industry which specialises in Green Energy Solutions. She is on a mission to save nature and Mother Earth. This company has been awarded as "The Most Trusted Startup Solar Company in Delhi" by Bollywood Actor Sonu Sood and one more award to this startup as " Emerging Startup of the year" from the Global Business Icon.

Neelam has been awarded the prestigious "Mahila Krishak Samman" by Mr. Kailash Choudhary (Union Minister of State for Agriculture and Farmers' Welfare, Government of India | MP) and has been awarded "Women Icon 2022" by the Nari Shakti Foundation. In 2022, she got selected by IIM Banglore for an Entrepreneurship degree for Goldman Sachs.

As she automated her Green Startup, so Neelam spends some of her time with her NGO (ceNdor foundation) work, which help and support youth for education & more new startups, for which she has been awarded as "Social Philanthropist of the year". Apart from this, She also love to spend time and energy in her new venture of food business Wisdombell Services Pvt Ltd, known as Bluetick. A dreamer and achiever, Neelam loves to motivate and inspire people through her words and wisdom.

Keep in touch with Neelam via the website:
www.neelamsingh.in